2nd Edition

A Manual for the Modern Drummer

T0078968

Alan Dawson
Don DeMicheal

BERKLEE PRESS

Editor in Chief: Jonathan Feist
Senior Vice President of Online Learning and Continuing Education/CEO of Berklee Online: Debbie Cavalier
Vice President of Enrollment Marketing and Management: Mike King
Vice President of Online Education: Carin Nuernberg
Editorial Assistants: Emily Jones, Eloise Kelsey

Special thanks to Deb Dawson Mullins, Florence Dawson,
Deb DeMicheal Cain, Dave DeMicheal, and Frank Alkyer.

ISBN 978-0-87639-182-2

 **Berklee** Press

 Berklee Online

Study music online at
online.berklee.edu

1140 Boylston Street
Boston, MA 02215-3693 USA
(617) 747-2146

Visit Berklee Press Online at
www.berkleepress.com

DISTRIBUTED BY

HAL•LEONARD®
7777 W. BLUEMOUND RD. P.O. BOX 13819
MILWAUKEE, WISCONSIN 53213

Visit Hal Leonard Online
www.halleonard.com

Berklee Press, a publishing activity of Berklee College of Music, is a not-for-profit educational publisher.
Available proceeds from the sales of our products are contributed to the scholarship funds of the college.

Copyright © 1962, 2017 Berklee Press.
All Rights Reserved

No part of this publication may be reproduced in any form or by any means without the prior written permission of the Publisher.

CONTENTS

FOREWORD

Welcome to the genius of educator, performer Alan Dawson, dean of modern drum set pedagogy. His methods in developing hand-to-hand technique, 3- and 4-way coordination, reading, and overall musicality have been tried and tested. His former students are among the very elite in contemporary music. They are acclaimed performers, recording artists, and educators, representing a wide spectrum of stylistic genres. They all have been influenced by Alan Dawson: the man, the music, and the method.

I first met Alan Dawson via telephone and mail, when I sought out to study with him as a college student, after being honored as a recipient of a National Endowment for the Arts Study Grant. Unable to work out the logistics necessary for a temporary move at that time from Chicago to Boston, I sought out local teachers who had previously studied with Alan, namely Joel Spencer, Michael Adams, and Johnny Lane, who initially introduced me to the pedagogy represented in this text.

Later, as a graduate student at Rutgers University, I had the privilege of studying with Keith Copeland, one of Alan's most noted pupils. Keith further crystallized Alan's musical message and technical approaches in a more practical way, especially in regard to my own expanding performing and teaching practice at this time.

During this period, I began touring, performing, and recording with James Williams as a member of his Contemporary Piano Ensemble, Trio, and most notably the "Intensive Care Unit" (or "ICU"), which also featured saxophonist Bill Pierce and bassist John Lockwood, who all had an established history of performing with the legendary Alan Dawson. The varied stories and experiences that these gentlemen shared impacted me profoundly and ignited my desire to finally meet and study with the master himself.

I finally had the pleasure of studying with Mr. Dawson in the mid 1990s. By that time, I was a touring professional. What was most impressive about my time with Alan was the excellence in which he demonstrated every technique, exercise, and musical concept he presented. After each lesson, I was left in total awe of the high level of musicality in which Alan displayed on drum set and vibraphone during our lessons. I remember so vividly the technical command, balance, touch, dynamic shading, and phrasing that Alan consistently applied to every single measure that he played. It is this level of musicality and artistry that I am committed to presenting to my own students and future generations of players worldwide in my roles as professor, private teacher, clinician, and mentor, which is a direct continuum of Alan Dawson's legacy and gift to the art of creative music making. Additionally, I have fond memories of Alan and his wife Flo attending some of my Boston area performances, in which his graciousness, approving smile, and encouraging words are forever etched in my remembrance. I consider myself blessed to have had the privilege of studying with Mr. Dawson.

It is that high level of musical attention that I encourage those who pick up this book to apply to their studies, teaching, demonstrations, and applications. Simply stated, aspire to get the most music out of every single measure presented within the following pages. Make every note count in bringing these varied exercises and concepts in Alan Dawson's *A Manual for the Modern Drummer* to life, by employing sound musical choices in regard to phrasing, time feel, touch, dynamic shading, and style-appropriate balance between the limbs.

Musically Yours,
Yoron Israel
Assistant Chair/Professor of Percussion, Berklee College of Music

INTRODUCTION

This book is not meant for the beginner or the professional. It is meant for the intermediate drummer who knows how to read drum parts, perhaps has had some marching-band experience, is familiar with rudimentary drumming, and wants to learn what and how to play in a dance band. Undoubtedly, such a student will be interested in jazz drumming. That is for whom this book is written.

The aim of the authors is to give drummers a good foundation from which they can develop individuality and creativeness. But before drummers can grow as individuals and creators, they must first grasp certain drumming concepts as well as fundamental rhythms that the dance-band/jazz drummer uses. And that is what this book is about.

There are few exercises per se in this book; the market is glutted with books dealing with rudiments, speed-building exercises, fingering charts, and muscle-developing tortures. In the end, there is, of course, no substitute for daily practice and actual playing experience for building technique. We feel no need to include mechanical exercises. Our concern is music, not calisthenics.

This book is not meant for self-study, though it can be used that way. It is best studied with a competent instructor—one who has had dance-band or jazz experience.

And if there is a central core or general orientation in this book, it is music—the drummer and music. We feel that the drummer must be as good a musician as any other member of a music organization. You should know music, not just drumming, and you should be familiar with scales and clefs, and with harmony and theory. We strongly recommend that the student who aspires to be a professional dance-band/jazz drummer study as many areas of music as possible. Many drummers play other instruments—usually one of the mallet instruments (vibraharp, xylophone, marimba). It is not necessary to master a second instrument, but you should use it as means to bettering your drumming. It will make you more aware of musical values to incorporate into your playing. Your way of thinking about music will be different; you will think as a musician, not as just a drummer.

It should be understood from the beginning that, while there are many rhythms and examples included, this book offers primarily a basic foundation and is not a foolproof system for playing. In dance work and jazz, so many things are improvised on the spur of the moment that no book or instructor could possibly teach all of them beforehand. No drummer worthy of the name says, "In the ninth bar, I'll play Lick No. 7, and in the last chorus I'll use Rhythm No. 88." Music, especially jazz, is dependent on too many immediate factors to be worked out in such a cut-and-dried method.

Thus, anyone who would be a dance-band/jazz drummer must have an imagination. You must "hear" what will sound best. You must be able to inject feeling into your playing, for a drummer must be able to play with as much emotion as any other musician.

Besides imagination and feeling, the drummer must have good time; you must be able to maintain a steady tempo. No one has perfect time, but most top-flight drummers vary the tempo so little during a performance that it is not immediately noticeable. Young drummers often despair when they are told they rush or drag. They shouldn't. Speeding or slowing tempo is common to inexperienced drummers. A sense of time can be developed. Listening to good dance music and jazz and playing with competent musicians are two ways of developing this sense of time. Usually, the ability to hold the tempo steady comes with experience.

This book is divided into three parts. The first deals with fundamentals. The second is concerned with dance drumming. We hope these two parts will contain most of the material the novice dance-band drummer will need to know when going on a first playing engagement.

The third section of the book deals with jazz—a historical review of jazz drumming, a theory of the development of the jazz drum solo, as well as an introduction to hand independence, cross drum solos, and 3/4 and 5/4 in jazz.

Alan Dawson and Don DeMicheal

Boston, Mass.

September, 1961

PART I

The Fundamentals

In the past, authors of drum methods have been divided into two opposing camps: either the author assumed the reader knew much more than could be expected, or else that the reader never had held a pair of drum sticks before. We hope to avoid either of these pitfalls. We assume the reader knows how to read drum parts, but we do not assume a great degree of understanding regarding the ins and outs of dance-band/jazz drumming.

This first part, then, is included for those who want to start from basics and go from there. It includes the cymbal beat in all its interpretations; the use of the feet, alone, together, and with the hands; and the use of brushes.

Even if you are familiar with these fundamentals, it will do you no harm to review. Never be so advanced that you lose sight of that which is basic.

THE CYMBAL BEAT: INTERPRETATION AND APPLICATION

The dotted-eighth and sixteenth ♩. ♪ is used so much in dance and jazz drumming and causes so much confusion that it is primary to understand thoroughly just how this figure is interpreted. (Note: all the following illustrations are played by the right hand, usually on a top cymbal).

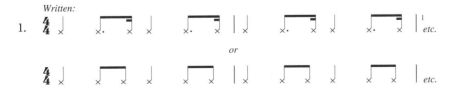

---

1 Cymbals are usually notated with a cross note ✗, but sometimes regular notes are used with a simple instruction written on the drum part that cymbals, often abbreviated cym., are to be played.

It is most often played as if it were written as part of an eighth-note triplet:

2.

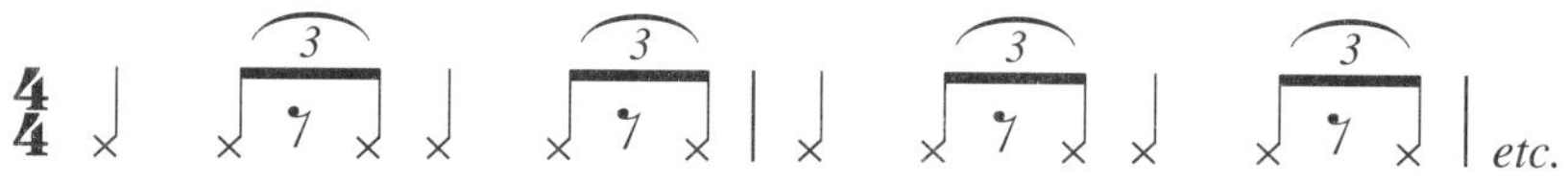

But there is no hard and fast rule on the interpretation of the figure. If the tempo is slow, many drummers will play it as notated:

3.

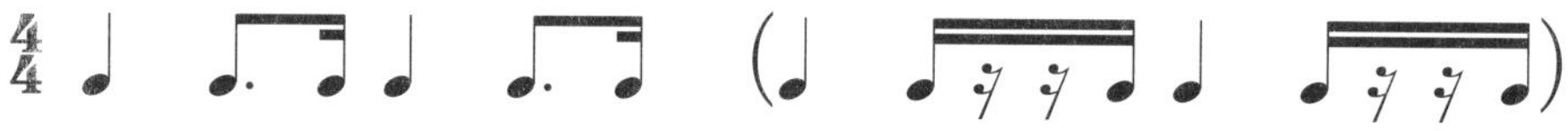

This implies double time and is often heard in jazz ballad performances (see part III).

If the tempo is extremely slow, the figure is sometimes played:

4.

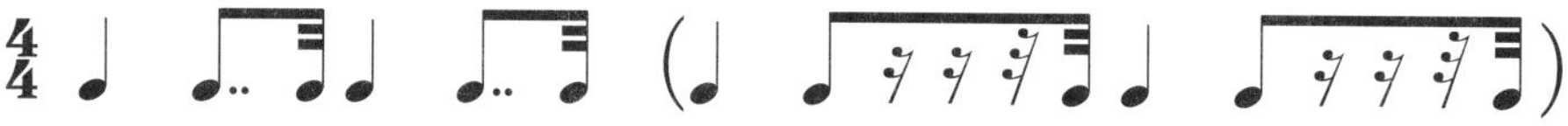

On the contrary, if the tempo is fast, most drummers play:

5.

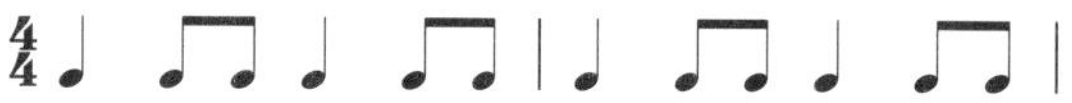

Sometimes the "sixteenth-note" of the phrase falls somewhere between the extremes of the last two examples. It is not possible to notate this accurately or clearly; it is more of a feeling than a notateable division of the beat. In general, as arranger Bill Mathieu has pointed out,[2] the space between the dotted-eighth and the sixteenth (using the term as a semantic handlehold) becomes greater as the tempo lessens. Mathieu devised the following diagram to illustrate his point:

6. 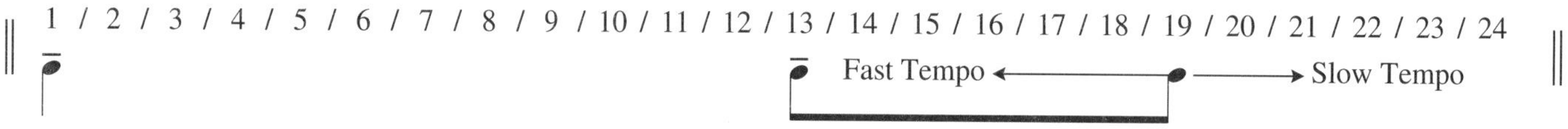
1 / 2 / 3 / 4 / 5 / 6 / 7 / 8 / 9 / 10 / 11 / 12 / 13 / 14 / 15 / 16 / 17 / 18 / 19 / 20 / 21 / 22 / 23 / 24

Fast Tempo ←————— —————→ Slow Tempo

Explaining the diagram, Mathieu said, "the unit is subdivided into 24 parts. The first note always falls on l; the second on 13; the third between 18 and 21 (depending on the speed of the tempo)."

The following example is designed to bring out the points concerning the amount of space between the eighth and the sixteenth. It is not meant as an exercise but as an illustration.

Start at a very slow tempo ($\quarternote = 50$), then gradually increase the tempo. You will find that at extremely fast tempos, it is impossible to have as much relative space between the two notes as is possible at a slow tempo.

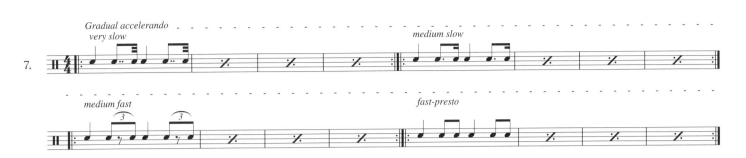

Since the top cymbals are so important in dance-band/jazz work, the drummer should choose them carefully. Most drummers use at least two of varying timbres. Many times, one of the cymbals is a sizzle (a cymbal with rivets, which produce a frying-eggs effect).

Different effects can be had from one cymbal by playing on different parts of it. Playing near the center produces a ping sound; playing midway between the edge and the center gives a fuller sound, but each stroke is still discernible. Playing at the edge of the cymbal results in a complete cymbal sound. This last method should be used with care, since, unless the rest of the band is playing fortississimo, the cymbal sound will overwhelm the rest of the music. The result is not music but noise.

PUTTING THE LEFT HAND WITH THE CYMBAL BEAT

Perhaps the easiest left-hand figure to play on the snare drum with the right-hand cymbal beat is a duplication of that beat:

Another simple combination of right and left hand is:

This is the first step to independence. When you can achieve complete independence of hands (the left plays one figure, the right another), you free yourself, as it were, and are able to create with fewer restrictions. We will deal more with independence later, in part III.

The following is a common and simple combination of left and right hands:

The left on 2 and 4 is played at different volumes for different effects. When played forcefully, usually as a rim shot, the above combination is termed a "backbeat."

But the modern drummer plays a more sophisticated left-hand snare-drum part than the above illustrations. Below are a few simple examples, but you should improvise your own after you have grasped the idea of the right hand hewing to the cymbal beat and the left hand free to complement and support the rest of the band.

Think of the combination of the left and right hands as statement and comment. The right states the tempo; the left comments on the musical proceedings, sometimes supporting, at other times opposing.

Study the following examples. Play them at various tempos, interpreting the cymbal beat as before, and then after you have the feel of it, make up your own left-hand parts. (For more advanced combinations of left and right hands, see "Hand Independence," part III.)

With accents (do not accent the cymbal beat):

Always bear in mind that what you play in the left hand must make sense and be pertinent to the music. Don't get so carried away with your excellence and complexity that you forget what you are primarily in a band for: to keep time and to support the others, not to detract from their efforts.

BRUSHES

If you have followed the usual course of development—lessons and practice on a pad, snare drum playing with a school concert or marching band—you have become more familiar with sticks than you have with brushes. When beginning drummers first encounter brushes, they find—sometimes to their utter confusion—that to manipulate a pair of brushes involves a somewhat different technique than handling sticks.

The greatest difference between brushes and sticks (aside from the sound produced) is that brushes do not bounce, and whether they realize it or not, every drummer relies on the bounce of the sticks to get the stick up off the drum to start the next stroke. With brushes you have to get the brush up with no help from it. But with a few hours practice, the muscles and mind adjust to this small effort.

More important than the physiological readjustment is the psychological reorientation. Drummers think differently when using brushes than when playing with sticks. In dance-band/jazz work, drummers think less of cymbal beats when they are required to play brushes, and more of what to play on the snare drum.

Historically speaking, brushes came into use during the 1920s, but it wasn't until the middle '30s that they gained wide acceptance, to a large measure due to the work of Gene Krupa with the Benny Goodman Trio/Quartet.

Krupa played a brush stroke that was adapted from a press roll on the second and fourth beats:

13.

Since it is impossible to play a closed roll with brushes (it is possible, of course, to play a single-stroke roll and an open roll of sorts), the "roll" in the following examples is made by drawing one or both of the brushes across the snare drum from left to right or vice versa:

14.

Two variations of the "press roll" brush beat:

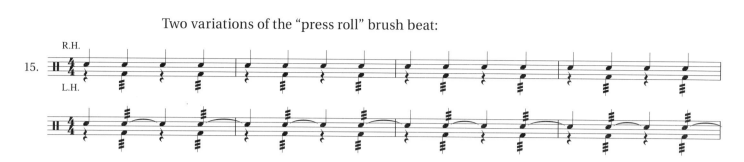

This beat, in its various forms, is still used, but for the most part, it is confined to society bands whose primary function is to provide simple and easily danced to music.

In the middle '40s, with the advent of the George Shearing Quintet, with Denzil Best playing drums, the abstracted press-roll beat gave way to what is now the more-or-less standard brush beat. I think of it as a swirl beat. In this figure, one of the brushes, most often the left, makes a full circle while the other plays the dotted-eighth-and-sixteenth figures discussed earlier.

Practice making this full-circle swirl clockwise and counterclockwise with each hand separately:

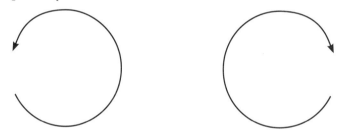

This swirl can be notated:

The novice may find that on the first few attempts, the swirl sounds scratchy—if it sounds at all. While seemingly a simple stroke, the swirl takes some time to master. (You may find that the brush wires catch in hair holes in the snare head; if this happens, reposition the drum so that the brushes miss these holes, or, if there are so many that you can't avoid catching your brushes, buy a new head.)

When you have mastered and smoothed your swirl, the next step is to apply what you have learned. The only function of the swirl—and this is one of the main raisons d'etre of all music—is that it produces a pleasant sound. But as pleasant as this sound is, it must be made of rhythmic value if it is to be of use to the drummer.

We combine the other hand with the swirl to give the needed rhythmic quality.

Below are the two combinations most often used:

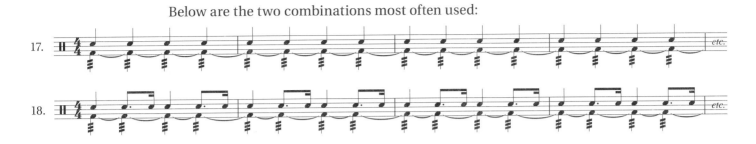

When combining the right and left hands, you will find—as drummers always do—several questions unanswered. Perhaps the most important at this stage of the game is: How fast do I make the swirl?

A good question, and one not easily answered with a "do this" or "do that." The speed of the swirl depends on several factors: the tempo, the desired musical effect, and what feels most comfortable to the individual.

The last factor cannot be dealt with by either book or teacher, but what to do for effects and what to do at various tempos can.

The swirl will, of course, be played more slowly at a fast tempo than at a slow one. It is impossible to make a full circle on, say, every beat at a very fast tempo, but this can be done at a slow tempo. Most drummers, whether they realize it or not, make a full circle every so many beats. More clearly, the brush making the swirl will be at the same position in the circle on the corresponding beat of each bar.

The number of circles per bar depends as much on each drummer's personal idiosyncrasies (what feels "natural") as it does on the tempo. But the speed of the circle or numbers of circles per bar should, except in rare situations, have a rhythmical relationship to the tempo: once a bar; twice a bar, if in 4/4; or one circle for each beat of the bar. (The latter is very effective if a tight[3] beat is wanted).

After you have the swirl and the various combinations in control, work on putting accents in the swirl for different effects.

There are several other brush beats. One of the more popular ones, among jazz drummers especially, is the following:

This differs from the swirl beat in that the left brush is shifted back and forth across the snare drum, as indicated by the arrows beneath the left-hand notes. The direction, of course, can be reversed. Usually, there is a slight push or accent on the second and fourth beats.

---

3   A somewhat unrelaxed, very precise way of playing.

This push-pull brush beat can be combined with the "press roll" beat to give the following:

20.

THE FEET

So far, we have dealt only with the hands, but the feet are as important—in some ways, more important—to the dance-band/jazz drummer. The student who has played only snare drum in a school band or orchestra will be at somewhat of a loss, the first time sitting down behind a set of drums. There is a great difference between patting ones feet on the floor and playing the bass drum (right foot) and the hi-hat or sock cymbal (left foot).

The coordination needed to play the bass drum and the hi-hat is acquired in only one way: practice.

There are two ways to play the bass drum: (1) when the beater ball strikes the head, hold it on the head for a fraction of a second; (2) when the beater ball strikes the head, release it immediately. The first deadens the sound by stopping the vibration of the head; the second lets the sound ring longer.

Likewise, there are two ways to play the hi-hat[4]: (1) after the cymbals have met, hold them together (by foot pressure), then release them; (2) after they have met, release the pressure immediately. The first is used most often; it produces a "chick" sound, while the second produces a "chang" effect. The second should be used only for effect, not as a constant rhythmic figure, except on very rare occasions.

After you have learned to play each of the pedal-operated devices separately, the next step is to combine them. Great care must be taken to make sure that the bass-drum beater ball meets the head at the very same instant as the sock cymbals close.

There are three simple combinations of right and left feet commonly used as time-keeping beats:

(= Hi-Hat, = Bass Drum):

21.

22.

23.

---

4   *Sock cymbal(s)* and *hi-hat* are interchangeable terms.

The third is not used nearly as often as the first two, but it is effective in certain musical situations.

Our point about two, sometimes three, combinations of bass drum and hi-hat should not be misinterpreted. (The phrase "time keeping" is the key to our contention.) This is not to say that there are no other combinations of the right and left feet. The feet, as the hands, can be combined in an infinite number of combinations.

Special effects for coloring and rhythmic novelty are desirable—if done tastefully and not at the expense of the tempo.

To develop each of the feet in turn, work out your own exercises like those following. (Interpret eighth notes as 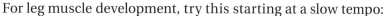 , as well as straight eighths.)

For leg muscle development, try this starting at a slow tempo:

Next, combine the feet in various patterns. (For this example only, the
hi-hat is written on the top line, the bass drum on bottom.)

Remember, these are examples. You can learn more by making up your own exercises, once you have the idea. It is not necessary to write out your own patterns. Your aim is to become a musician, not a machine. Improvise.

HI-HAT/SOCK-CYMBAL BEATS

Besides using the sock cymbals as in the preceding lesson, the drummer also plays on the cymbals with sticks and brushes. As a general rule, whatever can be done on a top cymbal can be done on the sock cymbals, but there are things that can be done on the sock cymbal that cannot be done as well on a top cymbal.

There are four main hi-hat/sock cymbal beats.

1. Keep the cymbals closed tightly, and play the basic cymbal beat near the edge of the cymbals. This will produce a sharp, penetrating sound.

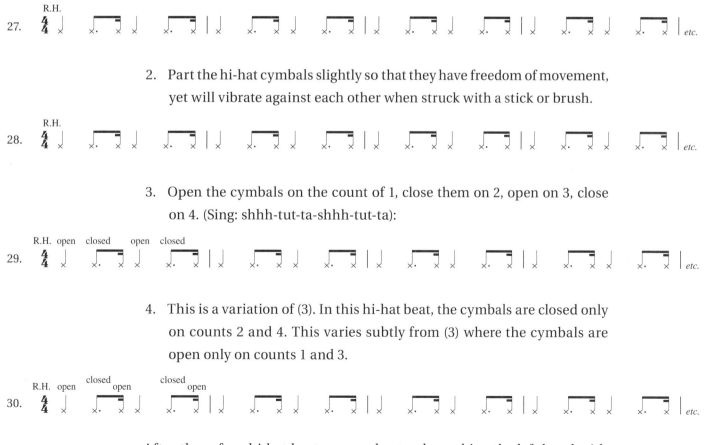

2. Part the hi-hat cymbals slightly so that they have freedom of movement, yet will vibrate against each other when struck with a stick or brush.

3. Open the cymbals on the count of 1, close them on 2, open on 3, close on 4. (Sing: shhh-tut-ta-shhh-tut-ta):

4. This is a variation of (3). In this hi-hat beat, the cymbals are closed only on counts 2 and 4. This varies subtly from (3) where the cymbals are open only on counts 1 and 3.

After these four hi-hat beats are understood, combine the left hand with each of them, as shown earlier when we dealt with the cymbal beat combined with the left hand. Go back to that section, and play the examples, only this time play the hi-hat beats instead of the cymbal beat.

COMBINING FEET AND HANDS: THE FINAL STEP

If you have followed our suggestions and advice up to this point and have put in long hours of practice mastering the various points and concepts, you should be ready for the final step that will complete your basic training: combining feet and hands.

Sometimes, you will be playing four related but different rhythmic figures. For example, here's a simple one:[5]

At this point, the right hand will be home base: it will play only the basic cymbal beat. Later, we will delve further into the intricacies of hand/foot independence (see part III).

Study and play the following, then improvise your own.

_____

5   Also practice and improvise on this lesson's points employing all the hi-hat beats. When using the hi-hat beats, disregard the sock-cymbal notation.

Dance-Band Drumming

Most drum methods slough off dance drumming, or are concerned with advanced drumnastics at the expense of dance-drumming fundamentals. This is all to the good—for the drummer who has learned dance drumming on his own by being pinioned on the point of sink-or-swim necessity. But one of our main aims in this book is to prepare novices for their first dance jobs so that they will not be run through and left to sink in the derisive jeers of their fellows. The mistakes drummers make on their early jobs often live many years to haunt them.

To do well in this field, dance-band drummers must be able to play whatever they may be called upon to perform—and this can be practically anything from a simple Viennese waltz to a complex show. When you declare yourself available for dance-band work, you must be prepared to play anything. You must expect the unexpected. The quality of the music you are expected to be able to play ranges from that devoid of emotion and consisting for the most part of mechanical timekeeping to that bordering on art. Between these extremes lie many forms and types of music, each requiring a different rhythmic approach, a different role for the drummer to fill.

Young drummers usually fall under the spell of jazz somewhere between the time they first become interested in music and their first professional club date. There is no better training ground for the prospective dance-band or all-around drummer than jazz. Nothing hones your rhythmic acuteness to such a fine point or fires your imagination to such limits as does jazz.

But that first dance job can be a shock if your listening and fun-playing are limited to jazz. Not only will you be ill-prepared musically, but your psychological preparation will be almost nil. To such a scantily prepared drummer, this first exposure to the music business, as it is, is normally not traumatic, however, and most of the fledglings pick themselves up, dust themselves off, and adjust, usually with the gnashing of teeth and the uttering of curses. But one of the facts of music life is that not all bands are jazz orientated.

As a general guide to dance drumming, the authors offer these bits of advice. Some are obvious but are included for those who may not readily perceive the obvious.

PLAYING

- *Be able to play in an acceptable manner anything* from Latin rhythms to all forms of jazz.
- *Always blend* with the rhythm section and the rest of the band. Don't overblow the others.
- *Practice on a full set of drums* as well as a practice pad. A pad is fine for building hand speed and endurance, but to get the feel of drums, you must practice an equal amount of time on your set. If neighbors or members of the household draw the line at full-set practice, there are simulated drum setups available, though these are not quite as satisfactory as a real set of drums.
- *Be able to play the bass drum.* Many young drummers ignore the bass drum, thinking it old-fashioned to play it as a time-keeping device. In certain forms of jazz, the non-use of the bass drum is accepted practice, but on dance jobs, it is expected that the drummer play with both feet. Besides, there is no guarantee that there will be a bass player on the job. In such situations, the drummer must provide the bottom of the band, and the bottom has to come from the bass drum. So learn how to keep steady time with your right foot.

EQUIPMENT

- *Use good equipment* and keep it in good condition.
- *Replace worn-out drumheads and sticks.*
- *When brushes become so misshapen* that they do not produce a clear sharp sound, *buy a new pair.*
- *It is usually not necessary to bring an elaborate set of drums* to a simple one-nighter; snare drum, bass drum, side tom-tom, hi-hat, cowbell, and one or two top cymbals are enough. If, however, there is a show involved, it may be necessary to include a floor tom-tom. Many acts require a simulated tympani effect, which is best obtained by playing a single-stroke roll with mallets on a large tom-tom.
- No matter what kind of job, *always set up in a position where you can see and hear everyone.* Get as close to the other members of the rhythm section as possible.

Although we have attempted to make this section as comprehensive as possible, it cannot cover all situations. Each job presents a slightly different problem to solve, some simple, some not so simple. Any drummers worth their salt never stop learning. You learn something almost every time you go on a job.

The examples in part II, as those in the first part, are meant as guides to general principles, if that be the right term for how to play a waltz.

METER

One of the basic factors of dance-band drumming—all forms of drumming, for that matter—is meter. By meter—there are several definitions—we mean the overall rhythmic construction of the compositions most often played by dance bands. Included in our definition of meter are the length of the composition and the time signature.

The length of these compositions fall into three large categories: twelve bar, sixteen bar, and thirty-two bar. There are, of course, many deviations from these three lengths (for instance, twenty-four bar, forty-eight bar, and so on), but the majority of compositions played by dance bands and jazz groups fall within the confines of these three.

The first, the twelve-bar composition, is the length of the common blues theme. Usually, the twelve-bar theme is repeated, making a total of twenty-four measures, but the basic theme is only twelve bars long.

The second, the thirty-two-bar composition, is the length of most popular songs (for instance, "Stardust," "Laura," "These Foolish Things," "I'm in the Mood for Love") and many jazz themes ("Perdido," "Bernie's Tune," "Scrapple from the Apple," "A Night in Tunisia"). Commonly, the thirty-two-bar song is one of two types: (1) the AABA construction ("I'm in the Mood for Love," "These Foolish Things") in which A is an eight-bar melody that is repeated before the bridge or release, B, which is a different melody, often in a different key than A, followed by a restatement of A; (2) two parts of sixteen measures each ("Stardust," "Laura") with a variation in the last two, four, or eight bars.

Note that the number of bars in all the various types of songs is divisible by two. The two-bar phrase is the cornerstone of most popular and jazz compositions. Most musicians, however, think in terms of four- and eight-bar phrases. Likewise, the dance drummer will find it more convenient when reading dance-band drum parts to think in terms of four-and eight-bar phrases rather than one bar at a time.

Following below are two typical dance-band drum parts. The first is from a typical stock arrangement, sold all over the country. The second is from a "special" arrangement. (The term "special" is used widely to differentiate between stock arrangements and non-stock arrangements.)

Stock Arrangement

Special Arrangement

Play

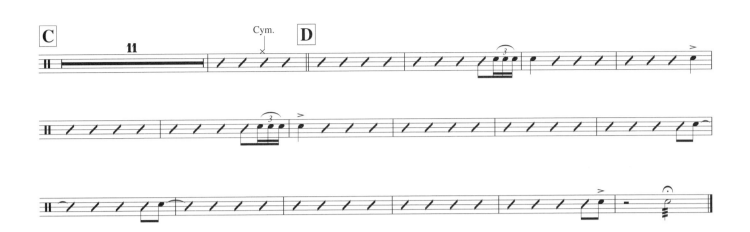

If played as written, both these parts would be dull. Nothing is said about the sock cymbal; there is not a dotted-eighth and sixteenth in either; in the second, there is no bass drum noted, not even that there is to be no bass drum played. Neither specifies whether the drummer is to play brushes or sticks. As you can see, much is left to the drummer's discretion in arrangements. (It may be that most arrangers don't know how to write for drums, but that shouldn't enter into this discussion.)

Most drummers, faced by these parts, would automatically fall into using ♩ ♪.♫♩ ♪.♫ instead of ♩ ♩ ♩ ♩. Most drummers would play the hi-hat on the second and fourth beats.

In essence, the usual drum part is a guide for the drummer, nothing more than a glorified cue sheet.

Note the great number of repeat measures. This is where the ability to think in larger units of measures is an asset. If you are used to reading the exercises in most drum books or playing the snare-drum parts in a marching band, you may have trouble keeping your place in the less-cluttered drum parts, typical of dance bands. It is essential that some method be used that will keep the place but not interfere with what is played. (If a drummer played the part shown above exactly as written, the result would be rather lifeless, to say the least.) One way is to count, 1-2-3-4, 2-2-3-4, 3-2-3-4, 4-2-3-4, etc. Another is to count, 1 , 2 , 3 , 4 , etc., each number falling on the first beat of each bar. But the best way is to "feel" four and eight bars without having to count them consciously. The drummer should be familiar with all these methods and be able to use any of them, for each will be handier in a certain instance than the other two.

A good way to learn to feel large units of time is to sing or hum the melody—silently or aloud—while playing the drum part. This "vocal" reading can be carried further by "singing" the drum part. This not only improves sight-reading ability (you "hear" the part), but will aid in developing a more musical, less mechanical, way of playing drums.

SYNCOPATION AND TIED NOTES

Generally in Western music, tradition has held that in 4/4 time the first beat is the strongest, the third beat next strongest, the second beat weaker than the third, and the fourth beat the weakest. In all time signatures, the first beat is traditionally the one stressed. Syncopation comes about when the strong beat or beats are made weaker by accenting the weak beats, or when accented notes (not the strong ones) are tied to unaccented ones, or when accented notes of long duration are placed between those of shorter duration.

No matter what the theory underlying accents and tied notes may be, it is essential that the drummer be able to read and execute syncopated passages.

Below are several studies utilizing syncopation. The accents are most important. The studies are meant to show the relations between notes and tempos. For instance, in the first three examples, if the first line is played at twice the tempo of the second line, they would sound the same. If the third line was played half as fast as the second, they would sound the same.

In the following, there are tempo relationships between the first and second measure of each line, and there are notation relationships between the top-line measures and those immediately below them in each two-stave example.

TWO-BEAT DANCE MUSIC

Although most American dance music is written in 4/4, much of it is played in
"two." This means simply that the two main beats of the bar are the first and
third. The reason that so much dance music is played this way is that it is suppos-
edly easier to dance to. There is also a psychological reason behind two-beat
dance music: it sounds livelier to ballroom operators and dance sponsors.

The function of the drummer in a two-beat situation is simple: you keep
time. You are not expected to create or embellish to any great extent. Often, you
are required to play brushes throughout most of the arrangement, using sticks
only on the last sixteen bars or so. This increase in volume makes it plain to the
dancer that the dance is about over.

There are several ways to fulfill this function. The most important thing the
drummer must include in time-keeping is an accent on the second and fourth
beats. This may seem antithetical to the inexperienced drummer, but that's
two-beat for you. There are several ways to get this afterbeat lift. One of the

most effective ways is to close the hi-hat on 2 and 4—close it sharply. By doing this and playing the bass drum on 1 and 3, the drummer achieves a boom-chik that keeps the dancers from getting their feet tangled.

The drummer can add to this by playing a top cymbal on counts 2 and 4. In some cases, the reverse sounds better—play the cymbal on 1 and 3 but accent 2 and 4 with hi-hat chicks and brush (or stick) accents.

Any of the brush beats in part I will do for playing two-beat music, though the first one ("press roll") probably is more in keeping with a "two" feel than the others.

In toto, the main thing to keep in mind when playing two-beat music (this does not refer to traditional jazz) is that you are not there as an artist. Collect your money and forget it.

THE DANCE-BAND DRUMMER AND 3/4[6]

The waltz is the most common rhythm in 3/4 that the dance drummer has to deal with. It is probably the most simple rhythm you will be called on to play.

In its simplest form, it is merely:

But there are several things that can be done with a waltz to make it more interesting. Simply adding a cymbal on the first beat of the bar perks things up considerably:

Many leaders insist on an accent on the second beat of every bar. This simple accentuation gives the waltz a lift.

Following are some combinations and variations of the waltz that are more interesting and more colorful than the first example given.

---

6   A discussion of 3/4 time in jazz is included in part III.

Brushes only:

All the above examples are meant to be played with the common, usually slow or medium-tempoed waltz ("Always," "Diane," "My Buddy," etc.). Most often, waltzes are played softly, and the drummer should use brushes, except when a strong lift is desired, such as in the last sixteen bars of a thirty-two bar waltz.

Another waltz form often played by dance bands is the Viennese waltz. It is played at a faster tempo than waltzes such as "Always." Sticks are generally used. There are several variations of the standard waltz rhythm that are used in Viennese waltzes:

Any or all these variations (and others that you can make up from your own imagination) can be combined with a straight waltz beat.

There are certain occasions when the drummer is called on to play 3/4 compositions in "one." This means simply that the tempo is so fast that it is easier to count one beat to the measure than three. This one count takes up the whole bar. Think of triplets when you have to play in "one" and play the first few bars as eighth-note triplets in 1/4 time until you can feel 3/4:

Another 3/4 rhythm the dance-drummer should be familiar with is the 3/4 (American) Paso Doble. (The Spanish Paso Doble is played as a 2/4 march.) The Paso Doble is usually played at a medium-fast tempo:

Note the bass drum.

LAME DUCK AND SHUFFLE RHYTHM

With the advent of rock, some drummers have found it advantageous to reach back into the past for methods of playing a suitable drum part for this music. Most of them went as far back as a heavy afterbeat and let it go at that. But there are more interesting things to play in such situations than a simple backbeat. Two of these are the lame duck (as good a name as any) and shuffle rhythm. Besides, once mastered, these two devices can be used in a variety of musical styles.

The main characteristic of the lame duck is the bass drum part. Below are the ingredients of this beat:

To give the lame duck a twist, play the left hand as follows. (Keep the cymbal beat going.)

Shuffle rhythm can be quite exciting in the right context. The right hand can play on a slightly opened hi-hat or a top cymbal, depending on the desired effect. The left hand plays the snare drum. Basically, this is a shuffle rhythm:

The bass drum is usually played on all four beats, the hi-hat on the second and fourth beats.

There are several things that can be done with shuffle rhythm to make it more interesting. Here are some possibilities:

It can even be combined with the lame duck:

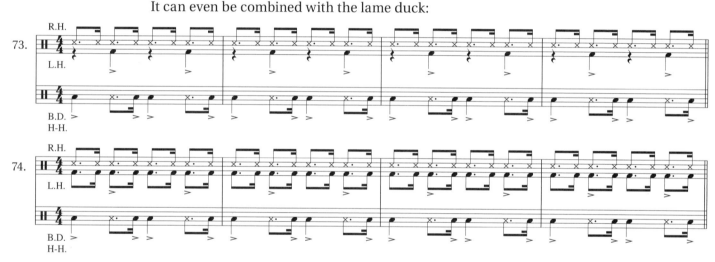

Another rhythm used frequently in rock 'n' roll is the triplet beat. Here are two variations. (The left hand accent is important; bass drum plays on all four beats, and the hi-hat closes on the 2 and 4.)

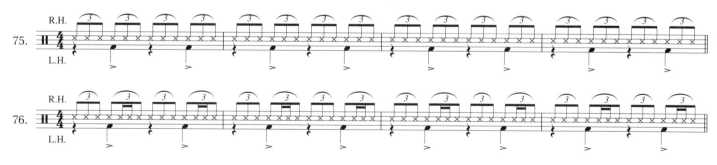

The second example is frequently heard in gospel-jazz performances. The triplet beat also is used in 3/4 (or 9/8) gospel-jazz compositions:

WORLD RHYTHMS

The variety of events the dance drummer is called on to play can be staggering. These occasions embrace tea dances, prom dances, shows, rock 'n' roll hops, society functions, midnight revels, waltz contests, and heaven knows what else. But one of the most confusing for the novice is the ethnic dance. There are in this country many nationality groups that cling to traditions of their cultures, including native dances. These range from the relatively simple-to-play polkas of Poland (usually all that is required of the drummer is keeping a 2/4, almost marching, rhythm going) to the odd, for our culture, time signatures of Greek, Turkish, Indian, and Armenian rhythms.

In all these odd-time-signature rhythms, there is a "hump" that serves as home base for the dancers. For example:

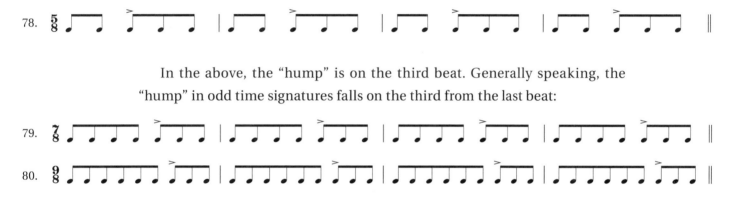

In the above, the "hump" is on the third beat. Generally speaking, the "hump" in odd time signatures falls on the third from the last beat:

The variations on the above rhythms are infinite. Below are just a few examples of Turkish rhythms:

Some prefer to count these time signatures in half time: 5/8 becomes $\frac{2\frac{1}{2}}{4}$; 7/8 becomes $\frac{3\frac{1}{2}}{4}$; 9/8 becomes $\frac{4\frac{1}{2}}{4}$:

Though we have discussed in detail only Turkish rhythms, there is similarity between Turkish, Armenian, Greek, and Indian rhythms.

LATIN RHYTHMS[7]

There is more to dance drumming than keeping time and adding embellishments for American-styled pop songs and jazz-flavored outings. One of the basic requirements of the dance-band drummer is to be able to play "Latin" rhythms.

Since the introduction of the tango in the early part of this century, Latin rhythms have gained increasing favor with dancers in this country—despite evidence that the majority of the dancers have little idea how to dance to this music. With the dancers' inadequacy in mind, too many drummers neglect learning the many Latin rhythms—to them everything is some form of rhumba. This is not only poor musicianship, but drummers who turn their backs on Latin rhythms are robbing themselves of a major course in their education.

Perhaps one of the reasons for this why bother? attitude is that the dance-band drummer can offer at best only an imitation of real Latin drumming. This, of course, is undeniable, since authentic Latin bands employ a battery of percussionists. But the American drummer can, with some imagination, come close to imparting the essence and flavor of Latin rhythms.

For instance, a bongo sound can be effected by a simple manipulation of the left stick. Hold the stick between the thumb and first finger of the left hand with the bead resting in the palm. Lay the stick across the snare drum (with snares off) so that the butt end extends about two inches over the rim; rest the palm near the center of the head. Using the bead as a pivot point (it does not leave the head), raise the butt end. Bring it down sharply on the rim. Result: an imitation bongo pop. This trick can be used for most Latin rhythms.

An important thing to keep in mind while playing Latin rhythms is the clave rhythm:

7   The term "Latin" is used here as a catch-all. Though it is technically incorrect, it will serve as a category heading.

This rhythm is the basis for most Latin rhythms; the other percussion effects are built on this simple foundation.

To get Latin effects, the dance-band drummer should have, besides snare and bass drums, a cowbell and at least one tom. Some drummers carry bongos or timbales (a pair of single-head drums used in Latin drumming), but most do not. Therefore, the first part of this section on Latin drumming is written with the average drummer in mind.

THE TANGO

The tango is probably the most simple Latin rhythm to play, especially for the student with marching-band experience. The important part of the tango is the accent on the offbeat of the fourth beat. It is most often played as a roll (a five- or seven-stroke, usually closed).

Almost always played at a slow tempo, the tango allows little freedom for the drummer. It is the most restricting of all Latin rhythms. But this is its positive feature: the repeating over and over again of a simple pattern becomes hypnotic.

The tango is most often played on the snare drum with snares on (perhaps adjusted tighter than usual).

There are two basic tango rhythms:

The accent on the roll should be heavier than the accent on the first beat. This second accent is optional. The bass drum can be played either of the two ways written above.

THE BEGUINE

The beguine, like the tango, is a simple rhythm, and though it is less restricting than the tango, the beguine must follow certain paths in order to retain its character. Its distinguishing characteristic is a heavy accent on the offbeat of the first beat. This is what restricts the drummer. This accent should be made each bar, or at least, it should not be absent too long.

Usually the beguine is played as a series of eighth notes. The offbeats of the second, third, and fourth beats are accented but not as strongly as the offbeat of "one."

The rhythm can be played effectively on the snare with the snares off. To add a more Latinish flavor use the left stick as described earlier (note sticking):

Below are some variations:

A soft and soothing effect can be obtained by playing the beguine with tympani mallets and playing on tom toms as well as the desnared snare:

THE BOLERO

(While not a Latin rhythm, the bolero is included in this section for the sake of convenience and because it is sometimes combined with the beguine, being played during the bridge of some songs. The term "bolero" here refers not to the Latin bolero, which is a slow-tempoed version of the rhumba, but to what for a better name can be called the French bolero.)

The bolero, properly used, is an exciting rhythm. The excitement stems from the repetition of a two-bar figure. Like the tango, the bolero becomes hypnotic.

The original bolero was in 3/4. French composer, Maurice Ravel used it to good effect in his *Bolero*, Ravel's most popular composition—to his great sorrow.

The French bolero:

This 3/4 rhythm was put into 4/4 by dance bands wanting an exotic effect. For instance, what would an enterprising band leader do with a song like "Temptation"? Besides, the obvious answer, he could have the drummer play an Americanized French bolero. Unfortunately, this is usually what happens. But value judgments aside, the bolero in the hands of dance bands is written as follows:

It is usually played on tom-toms or a desnared snare drum. Tympani mallets make it sound more exotic. Often, there is a slight crescendo on the triplets in the second bar of the phrase.

THE CONGA

In the late 1930s and early '40s, the conga became quite popular with American dancers. Squirming lines of men and women shaking their posteriors and kicking their feet was a common sight in ballrooms and night clubs. Though this dance (and rhythm) is not as popular as it once was, the student should be familiar with it.

The conga is played with a "two" feeling. Written in either 2/4 or cut time, the conga rhythm consists of two-bar phrases or patterns. The distinguishing characteristic of the conga is the heavily accented "kick" in the second bar of these patterns.

Here are three conga patterns :

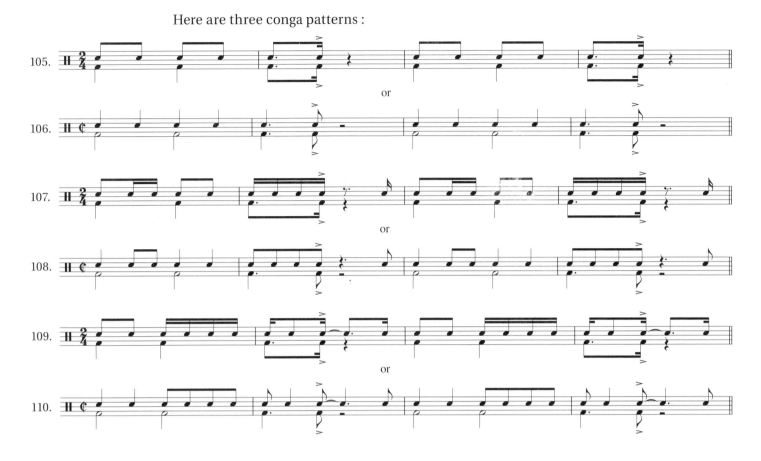

THE RHUMBA[8]

The rhumba and its variants, the guaracha and bolero, seem to be the most enduring of the Latin American rhythms. Less restricting than most Latin rhythms, the rhumba allows the drummer great freedom of expression, as long as that expression is Latin accented.

Below is a basic rhumba rhythm:

The accent on the fourth beat of the bar is important. Since the rhumba is usually played as a one-bar pattern (though each bar can be varied), this accent kicks the pattern and the dancers over into the next bar. It also serves as "home base," as it were.

Using the left stick as described earlier, and utilizing the full drum set, many variations are possible. For instance, the simple basic rhythm above can be played several different ways:

KEY: SNARE   COWBELL   CYM.   SM. TOM   LG. TOM   BASS DRUM   HI-HAT

8   For the sake of convenience, we use the term "rhumba" to include guaracha and bolero. They are basically the same rhythmic structure. Bolero indicates a slow tempo, guaracha medium, and rhumba fast.

When you get the feeling of the rhumba—when you think rhumba—improvise your own rhythms. You'll find the rhumba to be quite exciting.

Frequently, in the rhumba, and other Latin rhythms, the drummer uses a single-stroke roll, usually at the end of phrases. This roll is not the ordinary single-stroke roll; the left stick is played across the rim of the desnared snare (as explained earlier) and the right plays rim shots—not the usual rim shots, but, for lack of a better name, "little" rim shots. To make these little rim shots, the right stick should not extend more than two inches onto the head. Properly executed, this Latin roll should sound high pitched, similar to a bongo roll.

This roll can be varied by starting it slowly and accelerating until the maximum speed is reached right before the roll is ended on the first beat of the bar beginning the next phrase. Great care must be exercised when playing this variation; it should not throw you or the band. The time must remain secure. Never sacrifice time—no matter what you're playing—for effects. Never.

THE SAMBA

The samba is a Brazilian rhythm used originally to stimulate South American ladies and gentlemen to let fly their inhibitions. When it came north, dancers held onto their inhibitions, but the samba became popular anyway—at least, a mild version of it caught on with Americans.

The proper tempo for the samba is a medium "two." Most bands play it too fast, but then most drummers play the rhythm backwards, and practically none of the dancers perform the dance correctly.

The main thing to remember when playing a samba is to accent the second beat of each bar. This is what gives the rhythm its swing.

The samba can be written in 2/4 or cut time. Most often, however, the drummer is expected to fake the rhythm.

Below is a basic samba rhythm. Note the sticking; the left is played as explained previously. It is played on a desnared snare.

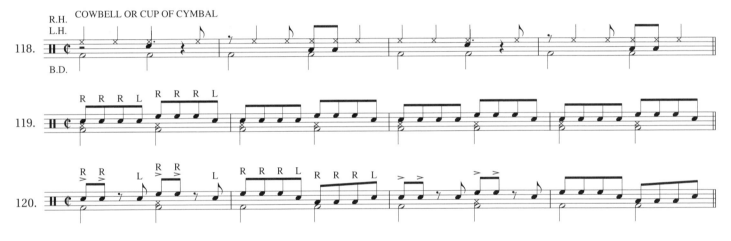

Played correctly the rhythm should sound "ah-gitcha, ah-gotcha." Play the first two rights near the rim closest to you. Play the second two rights in the center of the head.

A different effect can be had by using a brush in the left hand instead of a stick. Hold it in the usual way, but turn the knuckles up, and rest the palm of the hand on the head.

The samba is not as restrictive as the tango, beguine, or bolero; there's room for variation. By using the cowbell or cymbal and tom-toms along with the desnared snare, you can get several pitch variations:

As long as you retain the "two" feeling and get the emphasis on the second count, the drummer is allowed freedom in the samba.

CALYPSO

The calypso craze of the late 1950s has subsided somewhat, but drummers will no doubt run into situations where they will be expected to play a calypso rhythm.

The calypso comes from the French West Indies. In its pure form, it is a satirical song, the words of which are derived from social situations.

Played usually at a medium tempo, the calypso rhythms are built on this simple pattern:

This can be made more interesting by playing the left stick across the desnared snare, as explained earlier. Play the previous figure with the right stick, and play the left on the second and fourth beats:

The bass drum is played on the first, third, and fourth beats.

THE MAMBO

The mambo allows the drummer much freedom of expression, probably more so than any other Latin rhythm. The feeling of the mambo is similar to a jazz feeling. Usually, the mambo is played two ways: the fast-tempoed mambo and the medium-tempo version.

In the two examples below, the first is better suited to fast tempos, the second to medium tempos. The right hand plays on either the cowbell or the cup of a top cymbal. The bass drum (not shown) is most often played on the first, third, and fourth beats of the bar.

Next, incorporate two eighth notes beginning on the fourth beat:

Different drums may be struck by the left hand. For instance, on the second beat, play the small tom-tom or a bongo pop. On the fourth beat, play the large tom-tom.

When coordination of the right-hand improvisations and the left-hand basic rhythm has been perfected, improvise with the left hand. For example:

THE CHA CHA CHA

The most popular Latin American dance to grab hold in the United States in recent years has been the cha cha (or cha cha cha, depending on how authentic you care to be). The rhythm should be played at a not-too-fast tempo, since the dancers must follow an intricate pattern, the climax of which comes in the last half of the pattern—the "cha cha cha." This cha-cha-cha climax is played as three eighth notes beginning on the third beat of each bar—each bar in the beginning, at least, for when the dancers get into their routine, you can vary what you play.

Besides the cha-cha-cha characteristic, the rhythm has another distinguishing factor: most drummers use, and most band leaders insist upon the cowbell.

Below are several cha-cha-cha patterns. Use the left stick as explained earlier, even when the left is playing the cowbell because in these cases the left will move from cowbell to desnared snare.

THE MERENGUE

The merengue is a Dominican dance that has become popular recently. Originally, the rhythm was played on a tambour, a native drum strapped to the drummer so that it can be played on one head with the right hand and the other head with the left. Since most drummers do not carry such a drum as part of their regular equipment, the merengue rhythm must be played with the equipment at hand, in this case desnared snare, tom-tom, bass drum, and cowbell.

The basic merengue rhythm is played with a "two" feeling (usually slower than a samba tempo):

As in many Latin rhythms, the merengue is played in two-bar patterns. Occasionally, the above basic merengue rhythm is played in reverse, depending on the composition:

134.

The distinguishing characteristic of the merengue is the group of four accented sixteenth notes. These must remain constant throughout the selection. But what is played before these sixteenth notes can be almost endlessly varied. The merengue is also written in cut time.

Merengue variations:

In the above variations, the left hand can play on desnared snare or tom-toms. The right hand can play either the cowbell, cup of a cymbal, or closed hi-hat.

NANIGO[9]

There probably will be few occasions when you will have the opportunity to play the Nanigo in its pure form. But this African rhythm (it is included in this,

---

9   Nanigo is also known as "bembe."

the Latin category, as a convenience) is being used more and more in certain jazz arrangements.

It can be thought of as being in either 6/8 or 12/8, depending on the tempo (12/8 indicates a slow tempo). The feeling of this rhythm should *not* be the same as the more familiar marching band 6/8. Make the rhythm dance, not march.

Below are three nanigo variations. After you have the feel of this rhythm, improvise your own patterns—always, of course, retaining the nanigo feeling.

The right hand plays either the cowbell or the cup of a cymbal. The left plays on tom-toms and desnared snare.

LATIN RHYTHMS: TIMBALES AND FINER POINTS

Timbales come in pairs: two single-head drums, one timbal slightly larger in diameter than the other. The drum shells are made of brass. Timbales sticks are made from dowel rods. There is no bead, and they are shorter and lighter than regular drumsticks.

Many effects are possible with timbales. For instance, playing on the sides produces a high-pitched, penetrating sound. Incorporating the cowbell with timbales, or using a mallet in left hand and a timbales stick in the right, opens up many areas for sound variation. Or the timbales player can use bare hands for certain effects.

Below are two rhumba rhythms as played on timbales:

A cha-cha-cha rhythm as played on timbales:

The American drummer, when playing Latin rhythms, must improvise parts ordinarily played by six drummers in authentic Latin bands. In the following example, we will try to duplicate the sound of a separate cowbell player, a timbales player, and a congaist.

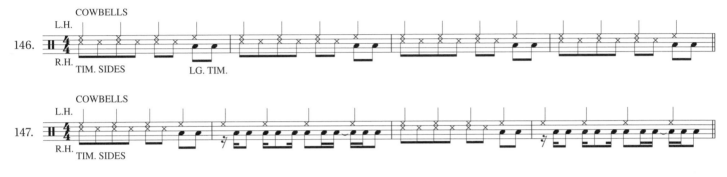

Bongo effects can be duplicated on the smaller timbal.

Occasionally in American dance bands, the rhumba will change into a cha cha cha for eight bars or even a full chorus. To the timbales player, the change is in the rhythm played on the sides of the timbales. Sing "Perfidia," and play the following:

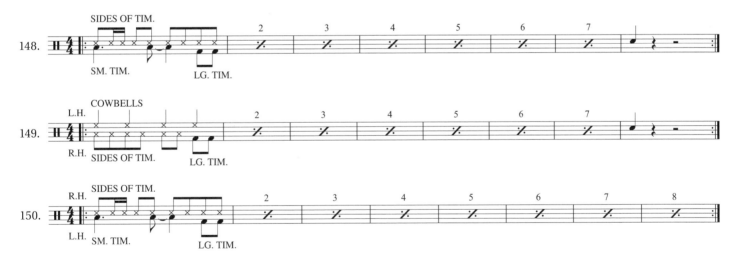

In the previous example, the first sixteen bars would be played in a more-or-less legato manner by the melody instruments. At the bridge (the seventeenth bar), however, the melody style would become more staccato.

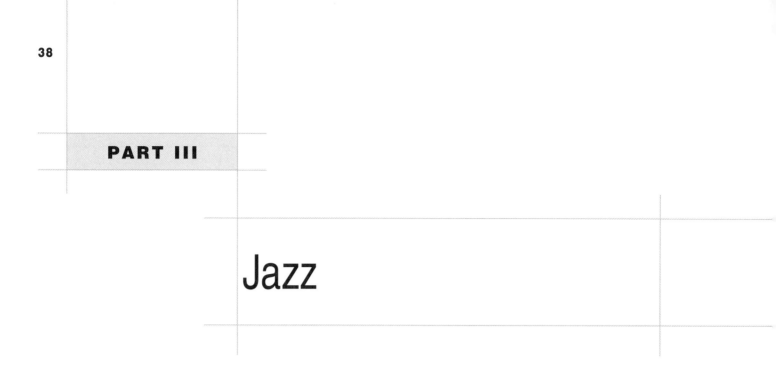

PART III

Jazz

(The following is reprinted from the March 3, 1960 issue of *DownBeat* magazine with the permission of that magazine.)

DRUMS IN PERSPECTIVE

By Don DeMicheal

Modern drumming is perhaps the most complex form of percussion work performed by one person in the long history of music. Surely, the modern jazz drummer is much more advanced technically and musically than his fellows of bygone eras. Aside from the technical aspects of drumming, the modernist is able to express a wider, more diversified range of emotions to his fellow musicians as well as to the listener.

Whence came this technical skill, this emotional diversity, this complexity?

They did not spring full-blown from the head of Zeus but instead have grown out of all that has gone before.

Jazz drumming has been with us long enough so that some sort of analysis can be made of its development. Viewing jazz drumming as a genetic, evolutionary process leads to some definite conclusions, and these conclusions may step on the toes of those who see jazz as a myth-filled and romantic folk art.

An evolutionary, historical approach requires pigeonholing men, concepts, and styles into eras; this is unavoidable and is for purposes of exposition only. The history of jazz drumming must be seen as a whole, as a growing, ever-changing phenomenon.

The germs of future developments are found in each era. Some men, such as Dave Tough and Sid Catlett, were active in two or more eras and changed their modes of playing accordingly. Others, for instance Sonny Greer, are of no particular school or era. Some well-known men will not be mentioned here, not because they are inept or forgotten but because their playing was or is to a great degree a reflection of others or their influence on the general character of jazz drumming was or is limited.

New Orleans and Chicago

A careful, prolonged study of early jazz leads to the conclusion that there was much more of John Phillip Sousa in the beginnings of jazz than an African tradition or echo of the jungle.

The idea that the Negro had some primitive "instincts" that raced heatedly through his blood when he first picked up a drumstick is a prejudicial racist theory. That the Negro is innately more rhythmic than the Caucasian is a myth; ask any drum teacher who has both white and Negro beginning students. If there is a difference in the rhythmic ability or conception between the two races, it is a sociocultural difference and not a biological one.

The Negro did, however, take the white man's marches and quadrilles and turned them into something far different—as much through negativism as through musical ignorance. For instance, the accents on the weak beats, which are found in the whole history of jazz drumming, can be seen as a negative reaction against what the dominant culture said was correct. But aside from the psychological overtones of early jazz, the important thing is that the Negro changed this military music into a thing of lasting and flaming beauty,

The rolls, flams, ratamacues, heavy bass drum, and other military trappings all can be heard in the work of the New Orleans veterans and their followers, the Chicagoans and the swingmen. This militarism, of course, was not left untempered. The pioneer percussionists added their own ingredients to concoct a dish unmistakably jazz. The unwavering stiffness of the march was softened and made flexible by changing the rhythmic feel from a strict 2/4 or 6/8 to one of 12/8 superimposed over a basic 4/4 time.

The most swinging exponents of this jazz-march style include Zutty Singleton, Ray Bauduc, Minor and Tubby Hall, Tony Sbarbaro (Spargo), Paul Barbarin, and Baby Dodds.

Dodds, in many ways, is the most satisfying of these drummers. He, more than any other, embodied the spirit and tradition of this military-flavored jazz. His work stands as a testament to the tremendous drive and swing this style can engender. Dodds' early recorded work with King Oliver, Jelly-Roll Morton, and Louis Armstrong is all but lost because of the primitive recording techniques of the '20s, but his beautifully subtle approach is well preserved on records made during the New Orleans revival of the '40s.

According to their own testimony, Dodds had a strong influence on the young drummers in Chicago during the '20s. Dave Tough, Gene Krupa, and George Wettling listened long and well to the young man hunched behind the ornate set of drums at the old Lincoln Gardens when King Oliver and his Creole Jazz Band played there. Thus, the military tradition was passed on and grew in adherents.

The Chicagoans added still more to the content of jazz drumming. The Chicagoans' most noticeable and positive contribution was a concern—sometimes overconcern—with technical skill. They experimented with cymbal effects and the bass drum. Instead of choking the cymbal as the New Orleans men did, they allowed it to ring; the bass drum beats were placed evenly on all four beats of the bar, instead of the first and third beats. The military hung on tenaciously with the Chicagoans'—especially Krupa's—reliance on the press roll and the rudiments.

The Chicagoans, at times, were guilty of some lack of restraint, but their unbridled enthusiasm was a joy to hear. The push and drive that they generated sparked many an otherwise dull recording session.

Swing

Chick Webb had a major impact on the drummers who heard him at Harlem Savoy ballroom during the late 1920s and through most of the '30s. Through numerous battles of bands, his dynamic work was spread among the drummers of the top bands who played opposite him. Webb's technical but subtle solos and his adroit cymbal work have been credited by more than a few drummers as having been of great importance to their playing. His devotees range from Gene Krupa to Philly Joe Jones. Especially significant was Webb's mark on Krupa's work, for it was Krupa who was to become the symbol of the swing era.

Krupa looms large in the evolution of drums, as much for his musical contributions—and they were many—as his popularization of the instrument. He brought to prominence a style that was in reality a further extension of the military tradition, tempered as it was by the dominant Dodds influence mixed with more than a touch of Webb.

His long drum solos with Benny Goodman, while mostly flashy and vaudevillian, at times contained much of musical worth. Krupa's work during the '30s with the Goodman trio and quartet, happily preserved on many recordings, was alive with enthusiasm, wit, and warmth.

Krupa's influence is almost immeasurable. His influence is discernible in the work of many who followed—even in the playing of such modernists as Max Roach and Art Blakey. The essence of his playing—the military—is most noticeable in his contemporaries of the '30s and those of later date who embraced swing. Stemming directly from Krupa and, in general, reflecting his approach are two of the technically most capable drummers ever to grace the jazz scene: Buddy Rich and Louis Bellson.

Rich is admired almost universally by jazz drummers, mainly because he has extremely fast hands and an ungodly right foot. This formidable technique rarely overcomes his powerhouse swinging and good taste. His influence, however, has been a technical rather than conceptual one. Bellson, a tremendous musician, has had little influence aside from his introduction of the novel double bass drum setup.

The perceptive jazz student will see that there is a vast difference between the basically military-oriented drumming of the swing era and the bop drumming that immediately followed. The key to this difference lies in the work of certain transition figures—titans when considered historically. Two were major influences, two minor. Let's look first at the minor, albeit strong, influences.

Cozy Cole was a mild sensation in the '30s with his Paradiddle Joe routine, but his contribution goes much deeper than novelty and popularization. His major addition to the jazz drummers' frame of reference was a technical one: hand and foot independence. He was one of the first—if not the first—to develop and master this coordination, which is such a necessity to today's drummer.

Simply, independence in its fullest form is the ability to play simultaneously four different rhythmic figures, one with the right hand, another with the left hand, a third with the right foot, and yet another with the left foot. Cole has developed this independence to an astonishing degree. On one memorable occasion, I heard him play not only four different figures at one time, but the figures also were divided between straight eighth notes and triplets. This is equal to holding two opposed ideas at the same instant.

Dave Tough's use and development of the top cymbal marks him as the other minor influence. Originally a Dodds follower—he absorbed the New Orleanian's message to an even greater degree than his fellow Chicagoans—Tough continued to evolve through the swing era. His work with the first Woody Herman Herd of the '40s not only drove that band to inspired heights but had a profound effect on jazz drummers as well. Tough employed larger cymbals than had been generally used previously, and their all-encompassing sound spread like a golden shimmer behind the Herd. More than any other man, Tough made the top cymbal the basic instrument of the drummer. His influence was so strong in the '40s that drummers were in danger of becoming nothing more than cymbalists. Fortunately, the excesses were conquered, and moderation in the form of a ping instead of a whoosh prevailed.

Sid Catlett and Jo Jones were tremendous forces in the evolution of jazz drumming—major influences because their contributions were more conceptual than technical. These were the men through which the military was subordinated to the orchestral. Drumsticks in their hands became the paint brushes of the artist, not the machine gun of the militarist. Both have been cited by leading modernists as having a telling effect on their playing. Traces of each man are heard throughout the modern drum world.

Jones is an attitude, a frame of mind, a feel. He injected into jazz drumming attributes that had been at a discount—relaxation, tolerance, and impeccable taste. More important than these even was the dynamic swing he brought to the Count Basie band of the '30s. Jones could lift the whole Basie band right out of the chairs with some simple but perfectly placed figure. His use of the hi-hat or sock cymbal never has been matched. Not given to flashy displays of virtuosity but content to integrate his playing with his fellows in a most musicianly way, Jones was and is primarily a group player.

Just as Jones pointed to a more musical way of thinking about the drummer's role, so Catlett pointed to a new way of thinking about the drummer's musical conceptions.

While he didn't escape the military influence completely, Big Sid developed a linearism rarely heard before him. His solos became percussive explorations of themes and lines in which one could almost hear the tune. Always a showman, he indulged on many occasions in the crowd-pleasing machine gun type of solo, but his really significant and lasting work is of the theme-variation type. Catlett showed that a drum solo could be a thing of beauty and as expressive as any other instrument's solo.

Nor was his linear conception the only contribution he made to the evolution of jazz drumming. His sparing use of the bass drum had its effect on those who followed, as did his very personal way of playing the hi-hat. He employed double-time extensively in his solo work, giving to the future still another means of expression. His bass drum explosions were echoed in the early work of the modernists.

Catlett's influence on the playing of Kenny Clarke, Shelly Manne, and Max Roach was not only great but highly significant; for these were the men who were the developers of what we know as modern jazz drumming. Thus, it can be seen what far-reaching effects Catlett's influence was to have.

Let's pause awhile before going into the modern era and consider the state of jazz drumming as it was at the juncture of swing and bop. From its beginnings, jazz drumming had evolved, picking up influences here, dropping others there, so that at this point, it had shed much of the military and had become more oriented toward the orchestral conception. Musicianship was, every day, more important; no longer could the idea of a drummer's not being a musician be accepted. The musical attitude of Jones, the independence of Cole's feet and hands, the cymbals of Tough, the linearism of Catlett, along with the technical advances of the swing men hung like storm clouds above the young aspiring drummers. When the storm broke, the young drummers didn't run for cover but reveled in the life-giving rain. The flood that followed was called bop.

Modern

Bop broke one of the last restraining links of the chain that bound the drummer to the military tradition—the bass drum. The bop drummer saw no logical reason for his duplicating the steady four of the bassist with his right foot; instead he used the bass drum as another tone color in his expanding spectrum of sounds. Time-keeping was confined to the top cymbal; later the sock cymbal, sharply closed on the afterbeats, was added as a time-keeping device.

Of major influence during the '40s and '50s was the introduction of Afro-Cuban rhythms to jazz. Dizzy Gillespie had much to do with bringing this element to the fore by using the congaist Chana Pozo in his big band. After an initial flurry of Cuban-flavored jazz, the Latin influence dissipated until about all that remains is a bongo pop that the modern drummer uses on the afterbeats at times.

Modern drumming is marked by a very intense, on-top-of-the-beat method of playing the top cymbal. Whereas drummers of previous eras used a basic rhythmic pattern | ♩ ♫♩ ♫♩ | ♩ etc., the new crop usually tightens this to 4/4 | ♩ ♫♫♩ ♫♫♩ | ♩ etc.

Manne, Clarke, and Roach stand out as the most important men of the early bop era. Although legend has it that Clarke originated klook mop or bebop drumming at Minton's in New York City in the '40s, this must be taken with a grain of salt when one considers the many forces at work at the time. Clarke's contribution was sizable, however, especially in the use of the bass drum, but was hardly as far-reaching as Manne's or Roach's. These two are still major influences and sources of inspiration and new directions.

Of the two, Roach was the more influential in the early days of modernity—even Manne was to a great extent in his debt. Roach took Catlett's style, added considerably to it, and developed one of the most dynamic ways of playing jazz ever has known. Perhaps his greatest contribution has been his experiments with time. Possessed of a remarkable sense of rhythm, Roach pushed back the barriers to free expression by such devices as superimposing 6/4 on 4/4, using groups of five quarter notes in opposition to four, and experimenting with 3/4 time. Roach has continued to evolve and follow new paths all through his career; today he stands in the forefront of modern drummers.

Many drummers enrolled in the Roach school; the most important one who has made contributions of his own is Art Blakey. Claiming to have lived in west Africa for a time and identifying with it psychologically, Blakey, more than anyone, has been responsible for injecting an African flavor into jazz drumming. His intense, exciting, and excited playing is marked by polyrhythms not unlike those heard in African drumming.

Stemming from Blakey, Roach, and Catlett is Philly Joe Jones—probably the most electrifying new drummer to come to light in the last five years and a strong influence on the young hard-boppers.

Manne, besides being an early influence, has been a major force in the development of neo-bop drumming—a "melodic" means of expression abounding in exotic flavoring and brilliant colors. Using mallets, brushes, sticks, silver dollars, and fingers, he has pushed back many tonal barriers. The duo album he made in 1954 with pianist Russ Freeman is a magnificent display of his melodic conception. Although this album was considered a pleasant novelty when it was issued, it may very well be one of the most important records affecting jazz drumming because it portends such interesting paths of expression.

The neo-bop, melodic conceptions of Manne have been augmented by Chico Hamilton and Connie Kay. Hamilton, especially, has added to the tonal effects of modern drumming with his exotic, always provocative work with his own group.

The steady rise in the level of musicianship undoubtedly will continue. The number of drummers who double some other instrument, who compose and arrange, has grown and will increase.

Quite recently, there has been an even greater freedom than bop afforded in drum solos. This development leads one to feel that we'll hear more and more free-style solos— solos not restricted by time signatures, meter, or tempo.

The finger technique (a way of controlling the sticks' rebound with the finger) so admirably employed by the almost-fabulous Joe Morello, will solve many technical problems, leading to fuller emotional expression.

TRIPLETS

Before going further into jazz drumming, it is essential that you understand thoroughly triplets and the triplet "feel" (really 12/8 time). Much of jazz, especially the earlier forms, and most of dance music is played with this feeling of triplets.

Below are a number of triplet studies, including the mixing of eighths and sixteenths with triplets. Play them with the thought in mind of getting the feel of the examples. One way of doing this is to "sing" the figures before playing them.

The studies are not meant as an obstacle course but as a help in grasping the almost unlimited possibilities of triplets and 12/8.

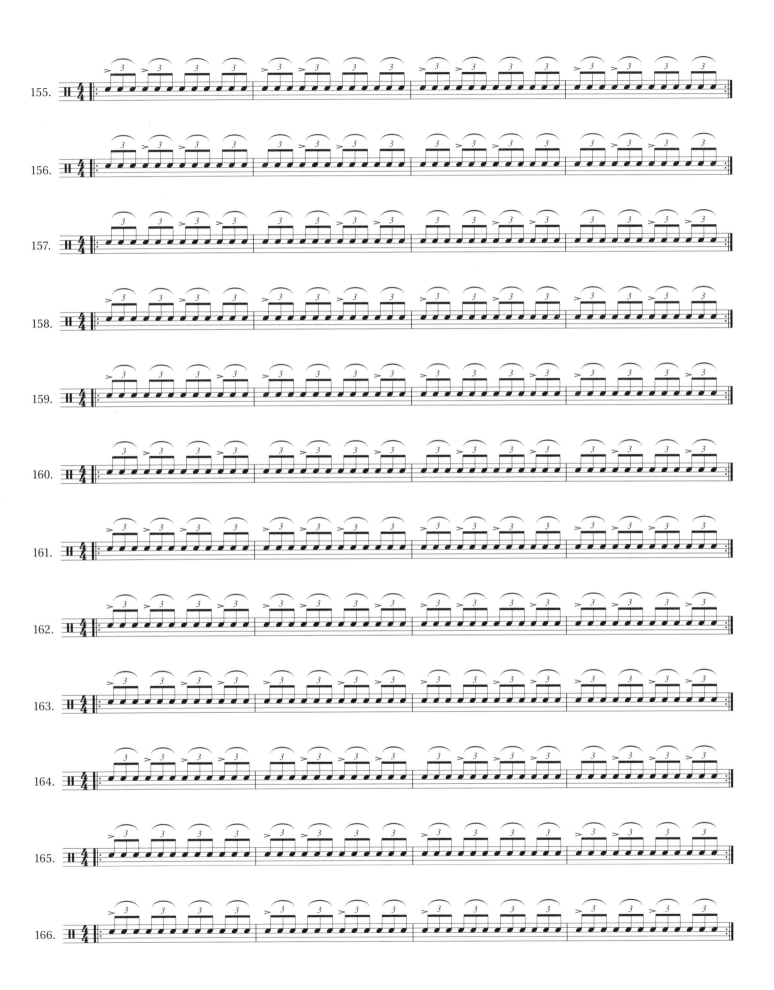

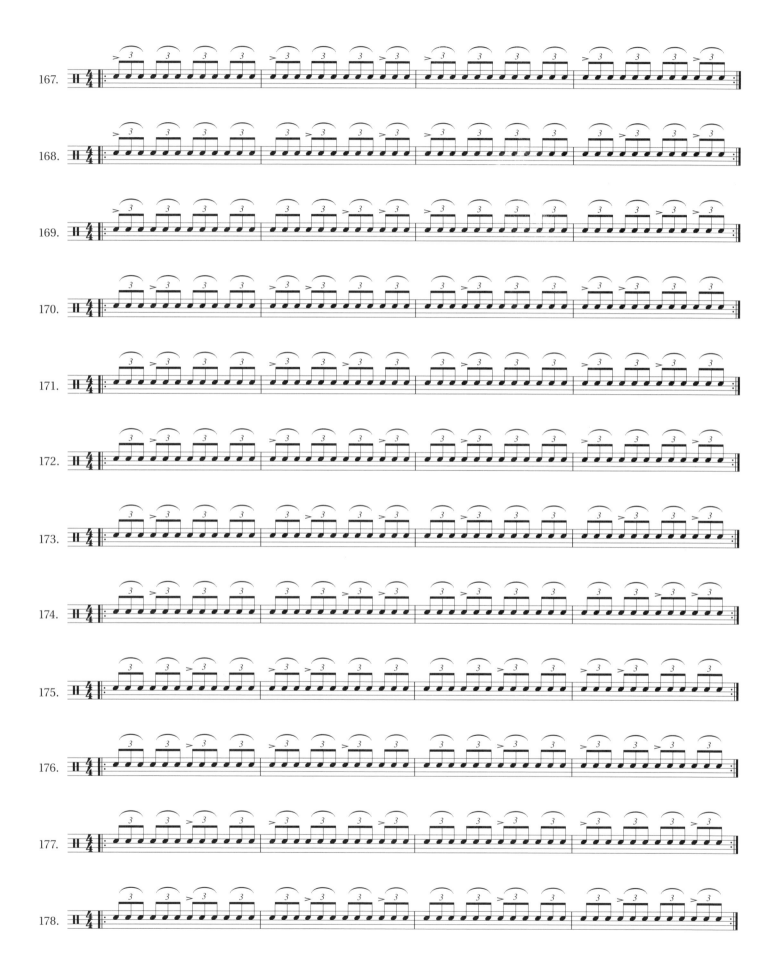

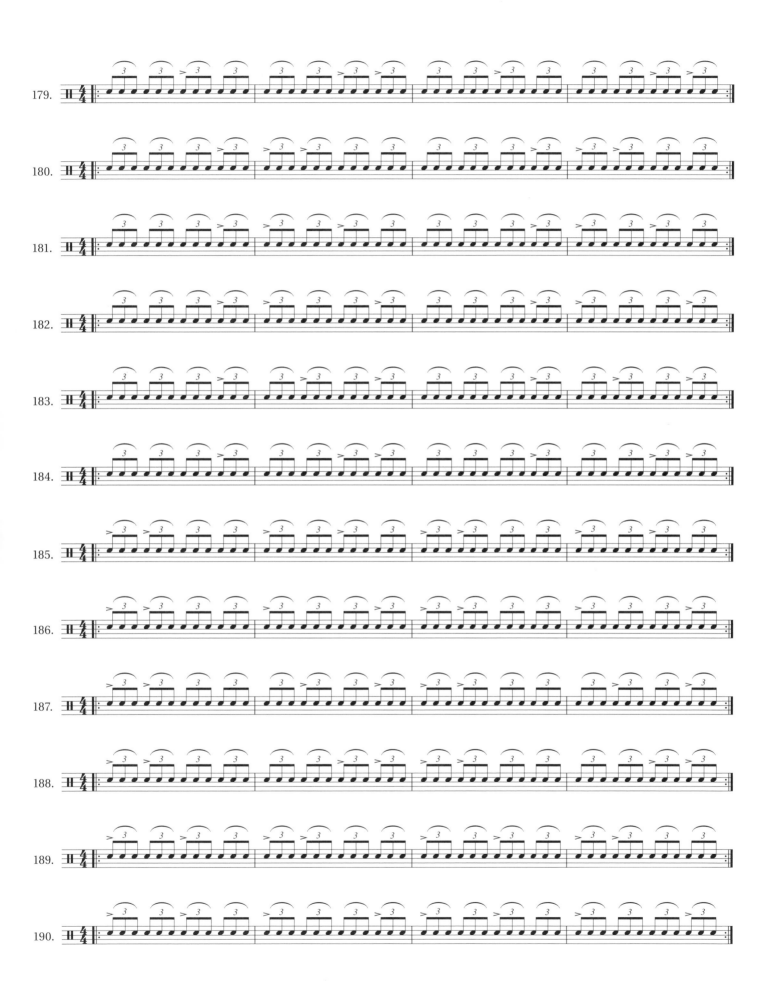

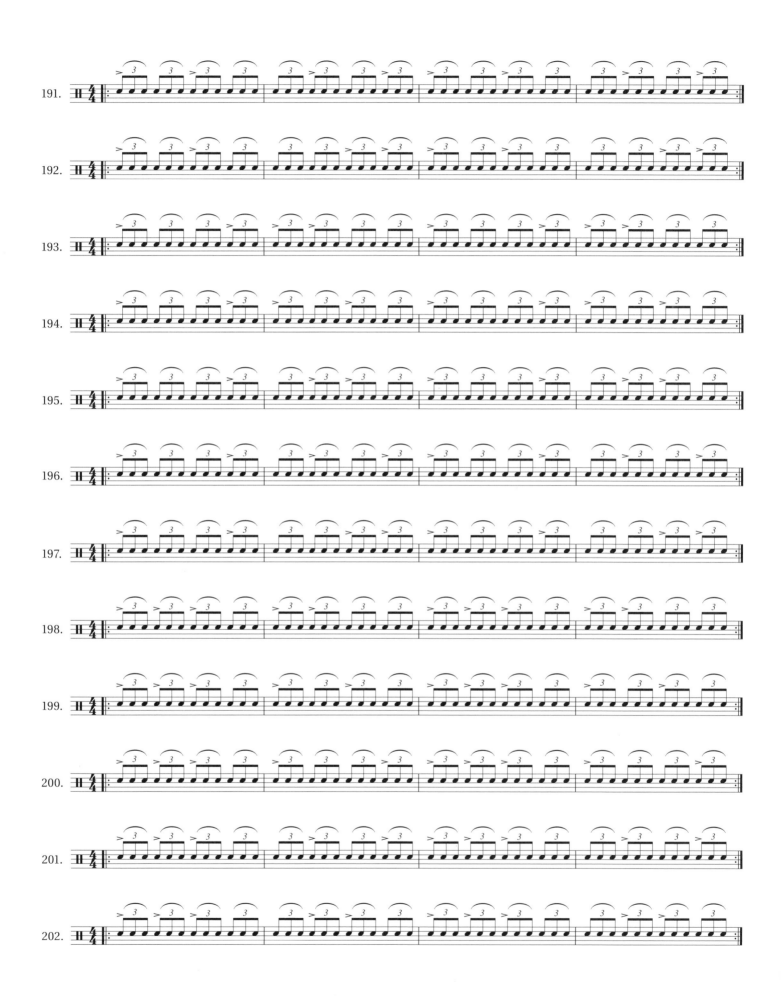

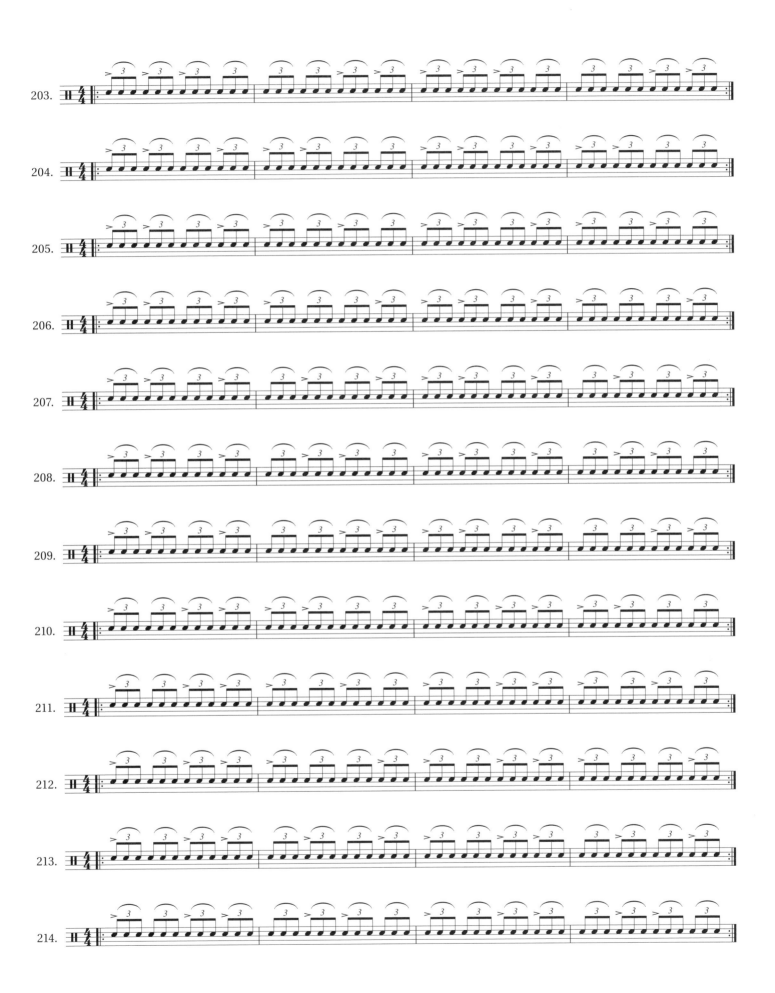

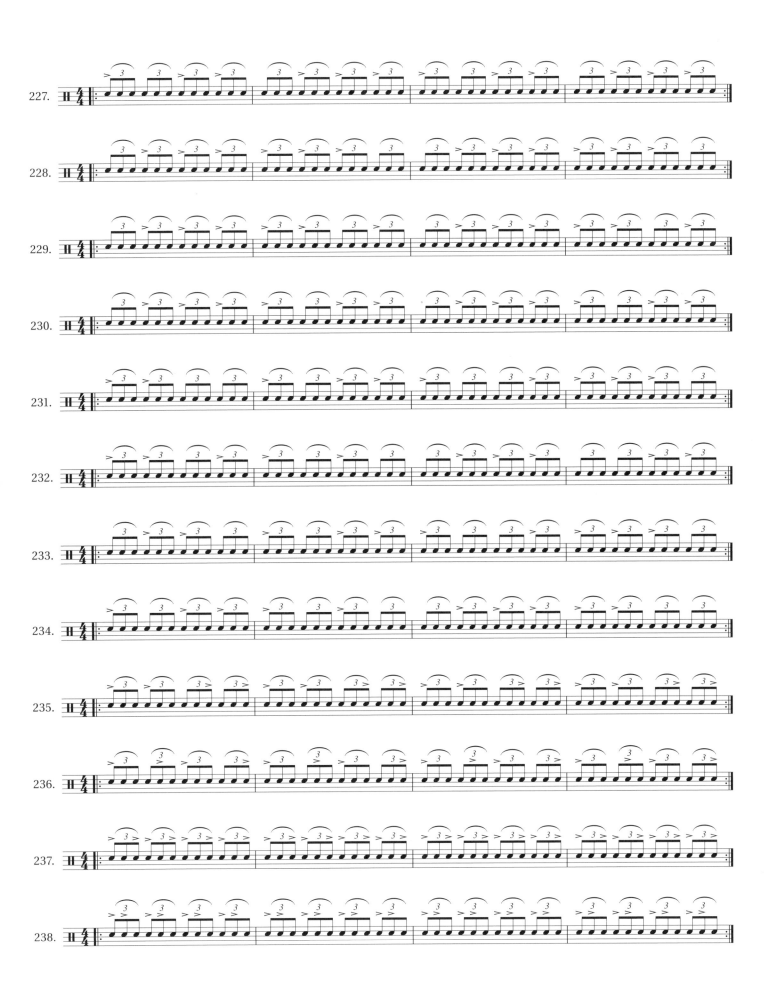

239. 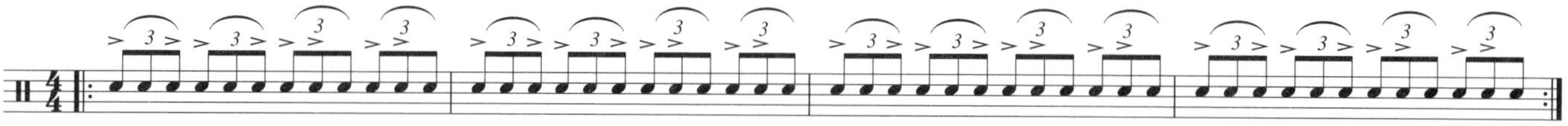

240. 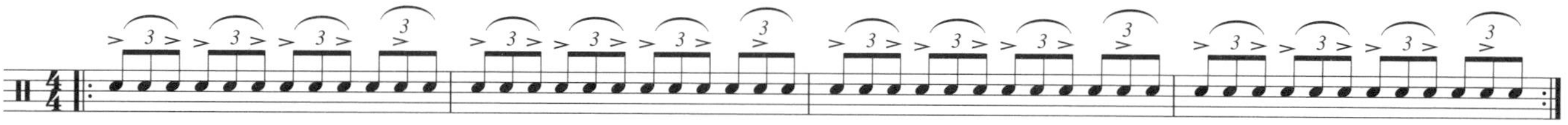

241. 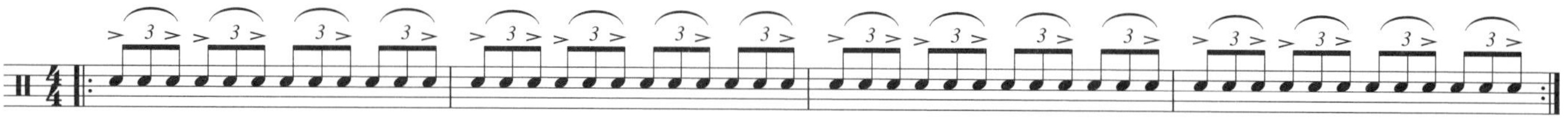

242. 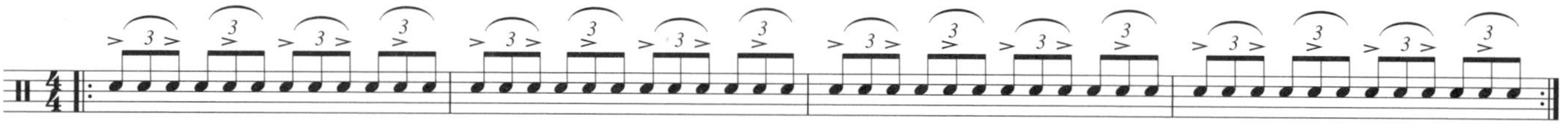

243. 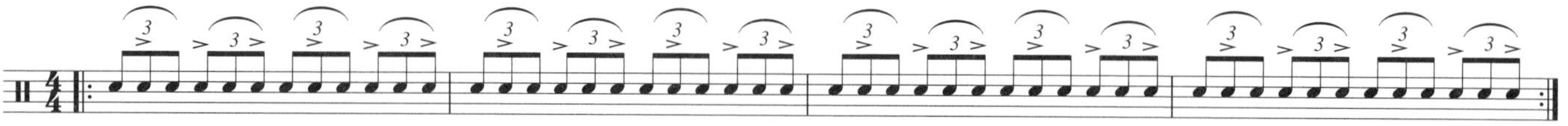

244. 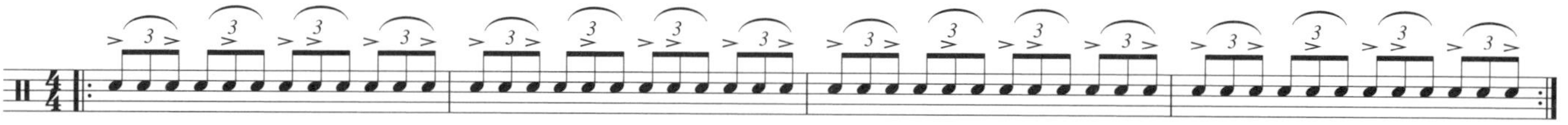

245. 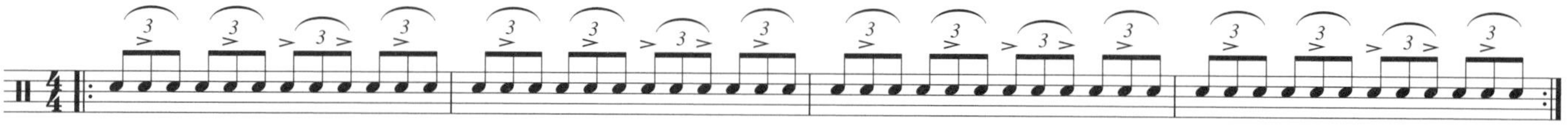

246. 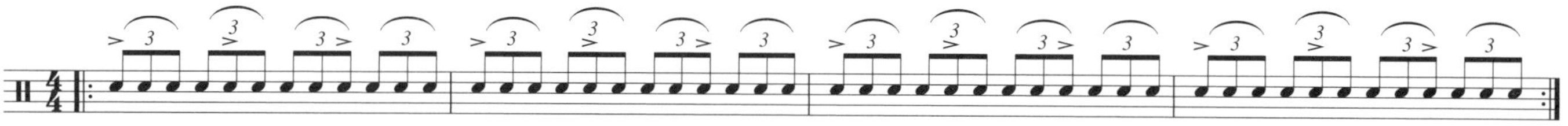

247. 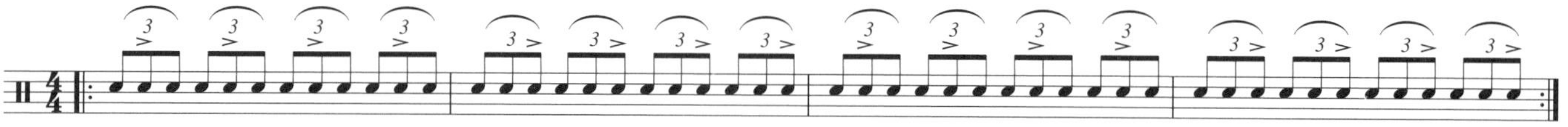

248. 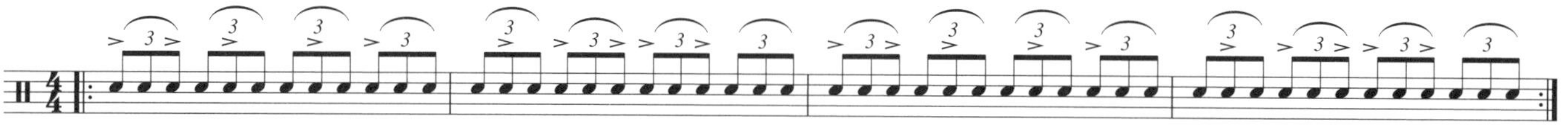

249. 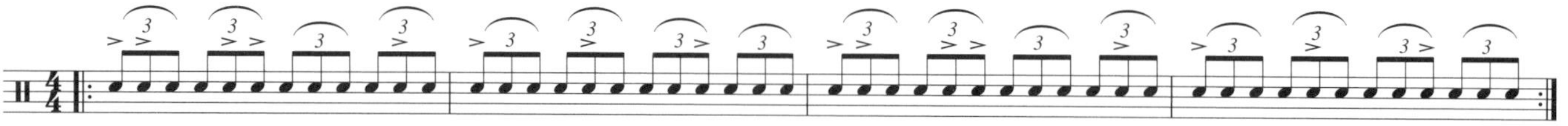

250. 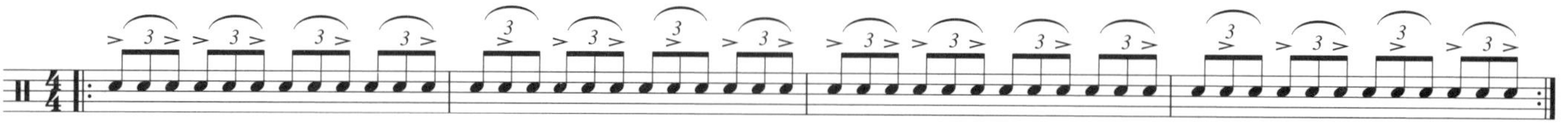

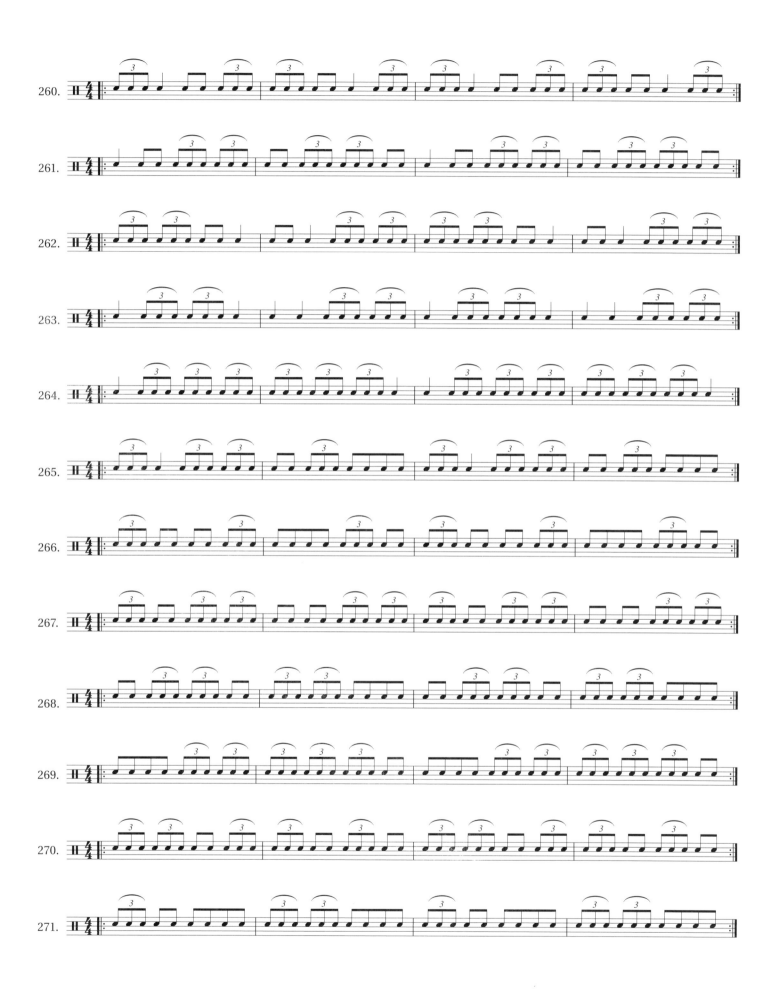

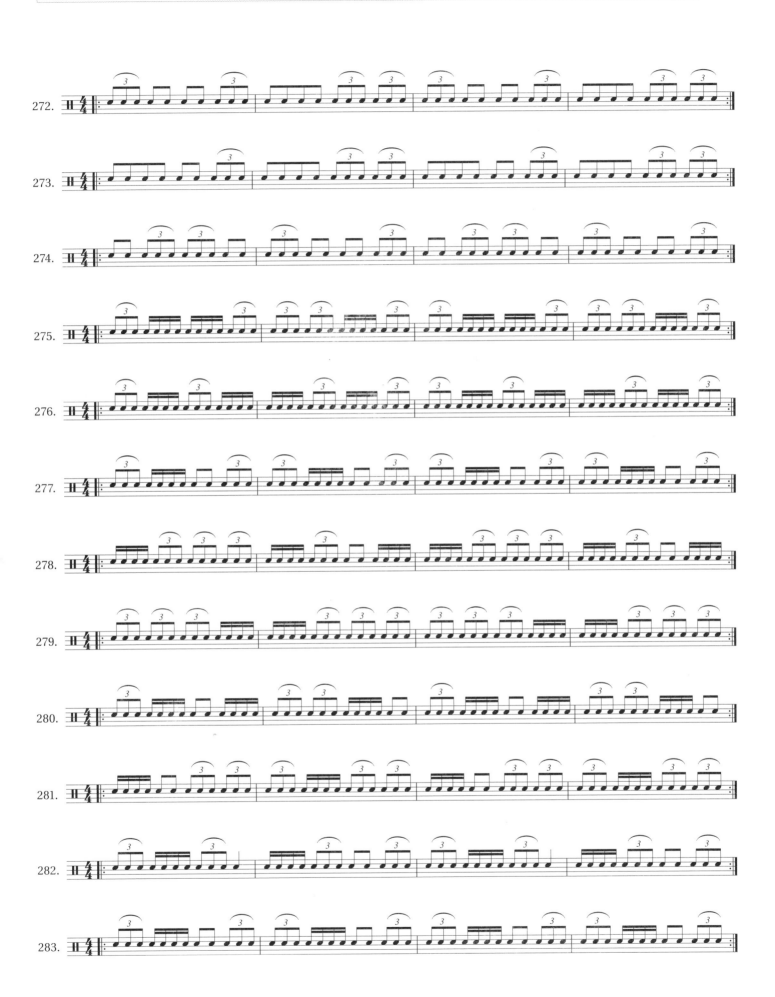

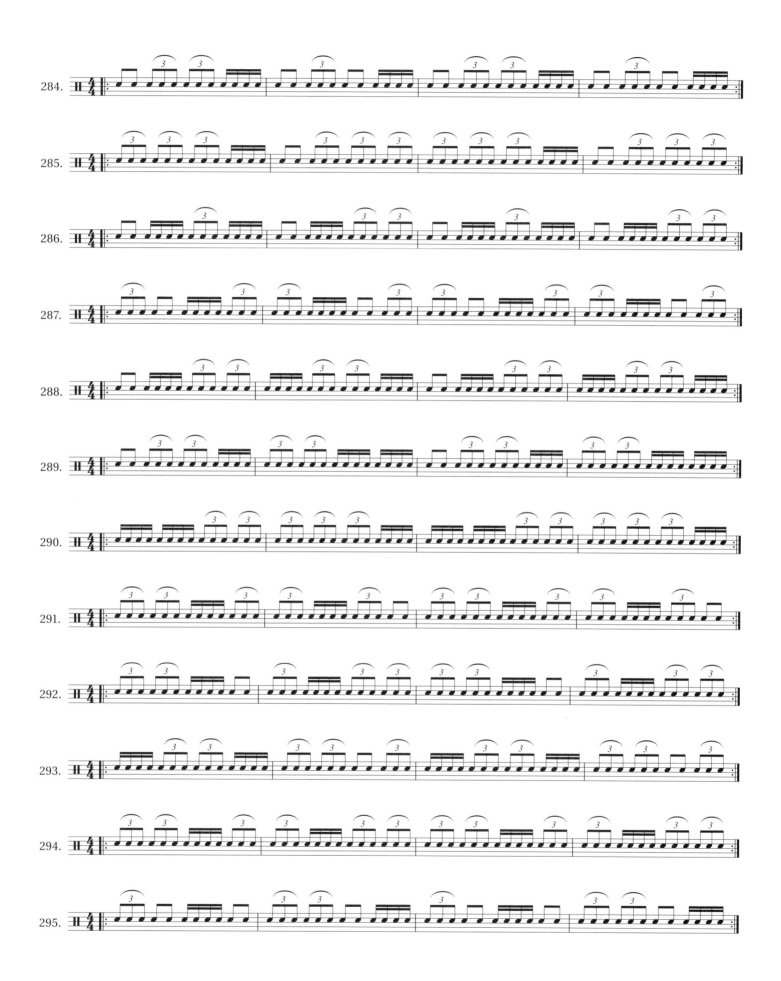

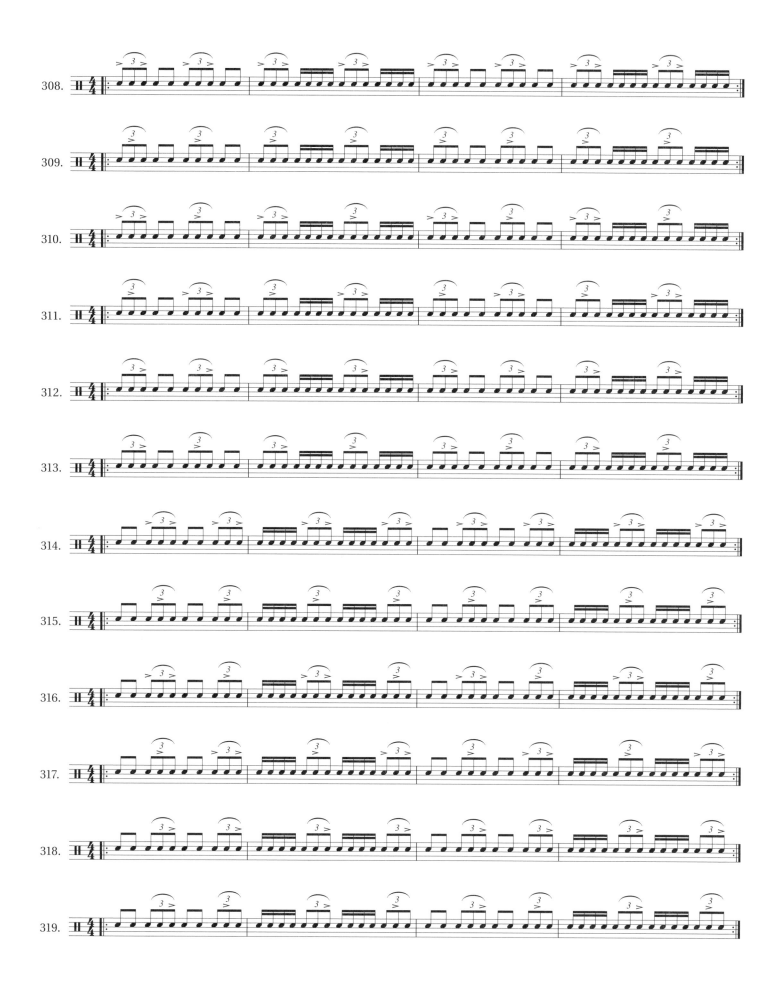

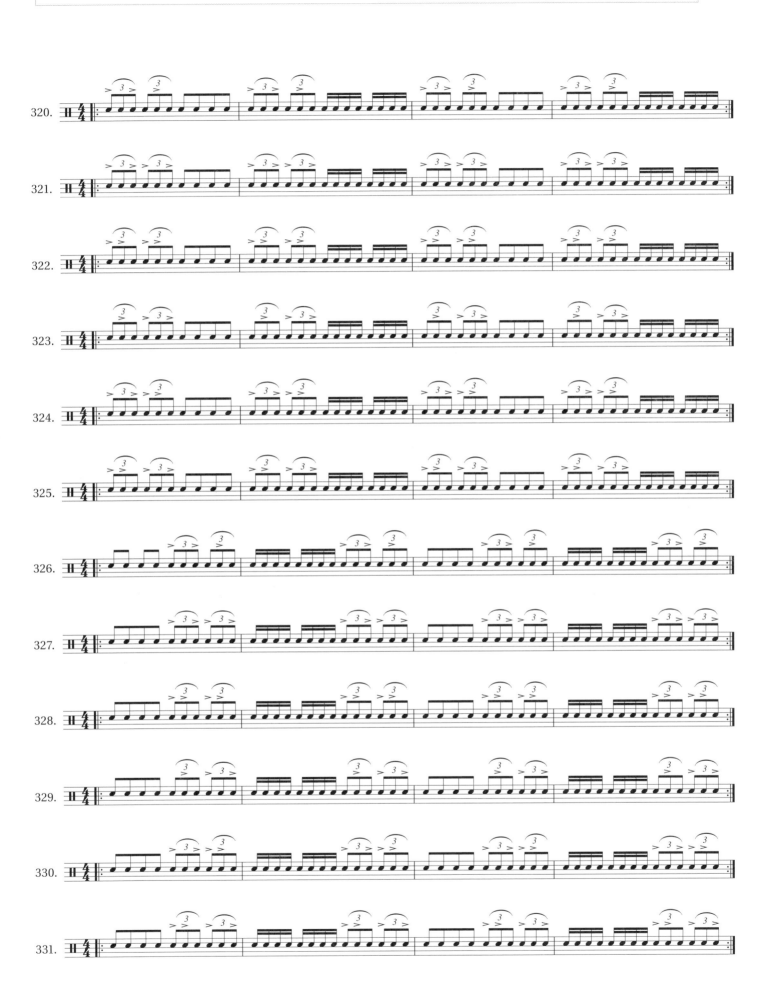

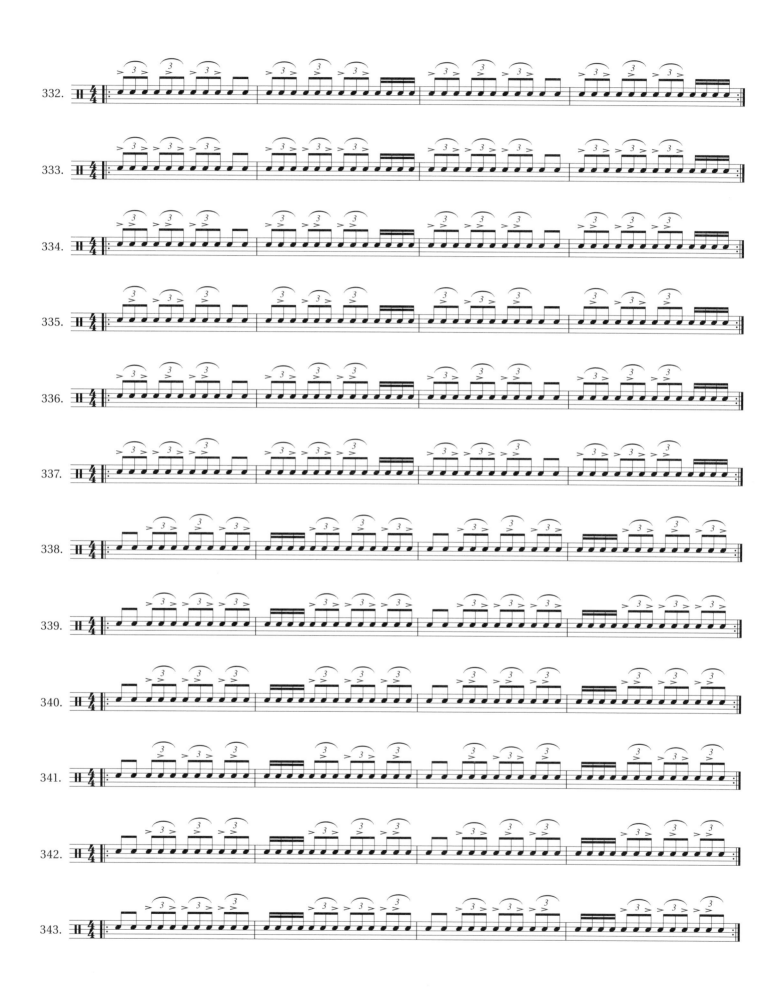

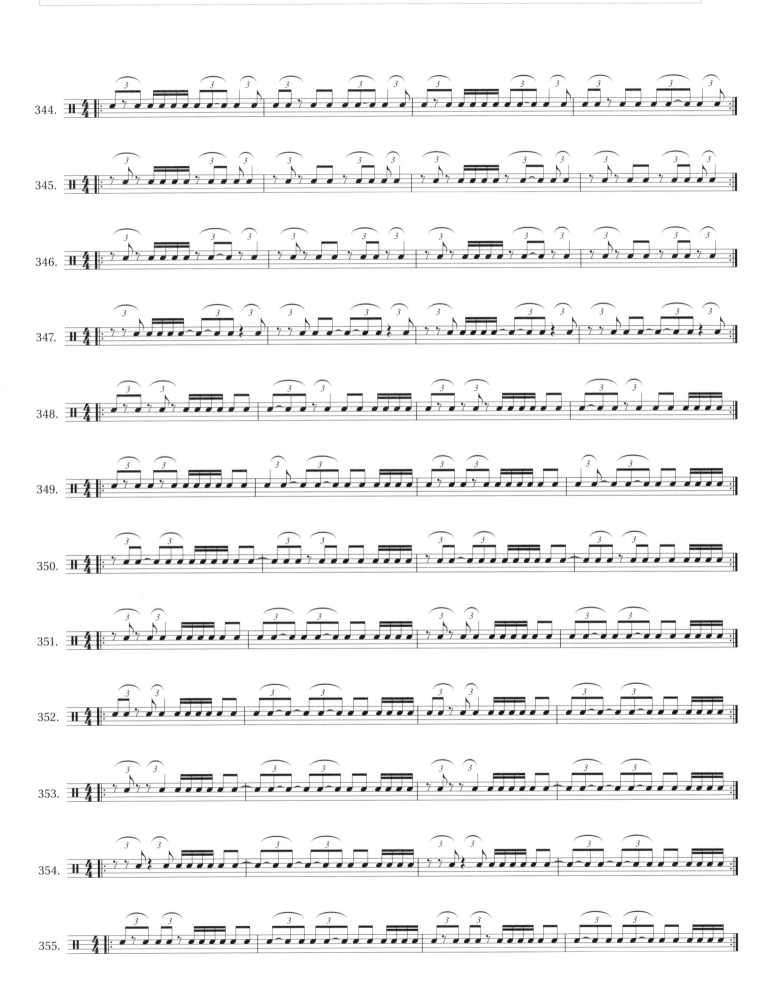

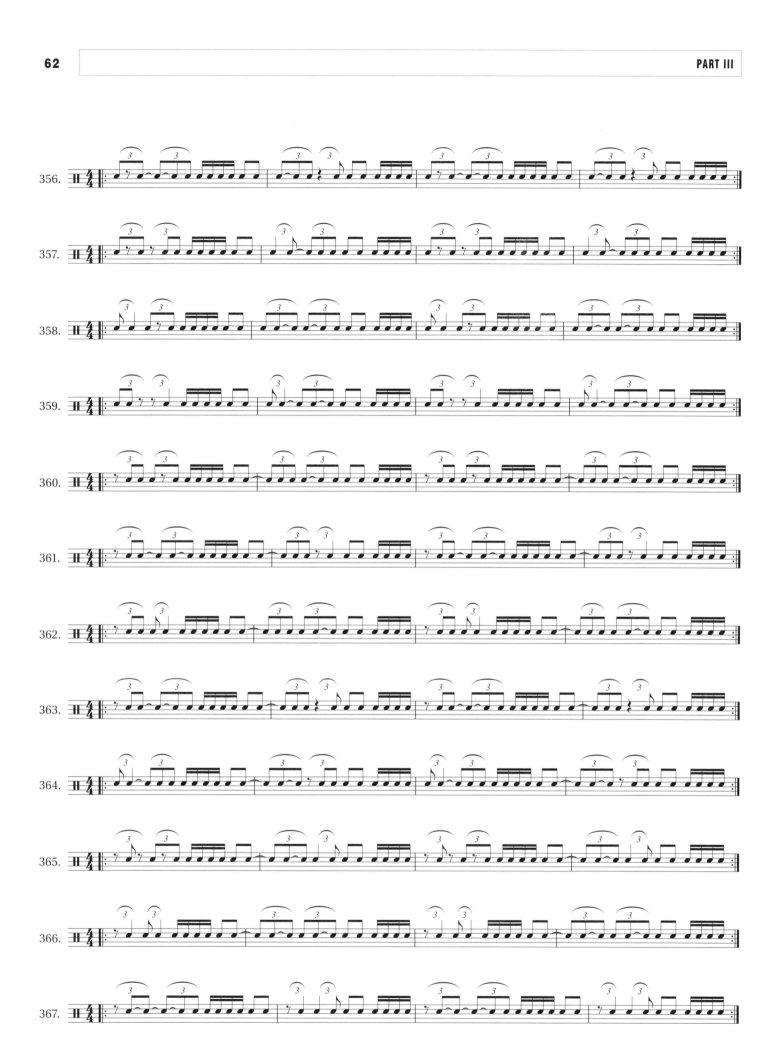

THE JAZZ DRUMMER AND DOUBLE TIME

Double time in the jazz performance is of relatively recent vintage, though drummers from the earliest era used double time on occasion. (Baby Dodds, for one, used it often in fills at the end of phrases.) But extensive use of double time behind a soloist during a slow- or medium-tempoed performance was not done until recently. Actually, what is referred to as double time is, in most cases, only half a double time—the cymbal beat ♩ ♪♩ ♩ ♪♩ remains constant but the hi-hat closes on the offbeats of each beat of the bar.

Written, modern "double time" looks like this:

368.

Note that the hi-hat does not close on the sixteenth note of the second and fourth beats, but combined with the dotted eighth-and- sixteenth figure produces an overall sound of ♩ ♪♪. Great care must be exercised when dropping out of double time. Don't let the tempo drop with you.

A word of advice: as the use of this double-time device has increased, so has the abuse of it. There are countless records on the market of a soloist playing lyrically on a blues or ballad, but the drummer detracts by double timing behind him. This device, as all musical devices, should be used in a proper context. If the soloist shows no inclination to double up, the drummer should not. There is no substitute for listening to what's going on. Play what the context calls for, not what is tricky or the supposed thing to do that month. Play music.

THE JAZZ DRUMMER AND "ODD" TIME SIGNATURES

Many have felt that if jazz were to continue to grow, it would have to burst out of what has been called the 4/4 trap. Until recent years, jazz had been played only in 4/4 (or variations of 4/4 such as 8/8 and 12/8). There had been only one experiment in 3/4 until the middle 1950s. That was Fats Waller's novelty, "The Jitterbug Waltz." And it was looked on as only a novelty, not as a vehicle for artistic expression.

Then, in the middle '50s, jazzmen began to experiment seriously with the possibilities of 3/4 in jazz. Much of this experimentation was done by Max Roach and Sonny Rollins. Since that time, 3/4 has become fairly common among modern jazz groups, especially during the gospel-jazz rage of 1960–61, although compositions in this vernacular are sometimes thought of as being in 6/8 or 9/8.

It is necessary when playing 3/4 jazz to forget about waltzes. The main emphasis of waltz time is on the first beat of the bar; this is not true in 3/4 jazz. Jazz drummers, when in 4/4, do not play 1 2 3 4/1 2 3 4. Nor when in 3/4 do they play 1 2 3/1 2 3. If jazz drummers anchored their playing to the first beat of each bar, the result would be a stodgy rhythm—an unswinging, non-flowing rhythm.

The accent in 3/4 jazz seldom, if ever, falls on the first beat; usually the second beat is accented.

Below are four examples of 3/4 jazz timekeeping rhythms:

Although the hi-hat is written on the second beat of the bar, it can be used on the third or on both the second and third.

Occasionally, jazz drummers play the same thing in 3/4 that they play in 4/4:

But this should be used sparingly.

The use of 5/4 in jazz is of even more recent vintage than the use of 3/4. Again, Max Roach was in the vanguard, though experiments had been done by others, most notably by Dave Brubeck, Paul Desmond, and Joe Morello. At this writing, 5/4 has not been developed to the extent of 3/4 in jazz. Many musicians feel that 5/4 will never swing, but there are just as many who feel that it is possible to make it swing.

There are also two ways of looking at 5/4. Most musicians think of 5/4 as a compound rhythm—a bar of 3/4 and a bar of 2/4. A few think in terms of the whole measure—five beats, not a sum of two and three.

However the jazz drummers think about 5/4, they usually play it as follows:

HAND INDEPENDENCE AND COORDINATION

Possibly the most valuable attribute a modern jazz drummer can have after time and taste is an ability to play one figure with the right hand and another with the left. This is commonly called hand independence. At root, it is really a matter of coordination between the hands (the feet, too). We have touched on this subject throughout the book, but these previous examples of hand independence were relatively simple.

The ability to play one thing in the right hand and another in the left enables the drummer to embellish without disturbing the flow of the time. Usually, the right hand maintains the cymbal beat; the left embellishes or, in some cases, underlines the punctuations of other instruments.

But this first exercise (yes, this must be looked on as an exercise) does not use the cymbal beat; it shows the relation of various triplets and quarter, eighth, and sixteenth notes.

First, six against four or three against two:

This can also be written as below. (The flam is not the military flam but indicates that the two hands hit simultaneously.)

378.

The following three examples will sound the same when played according to tempo markings:

379. 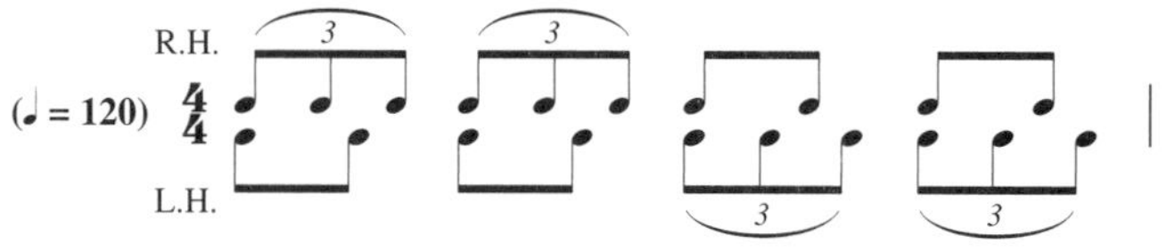 (♩ = 120)

380. 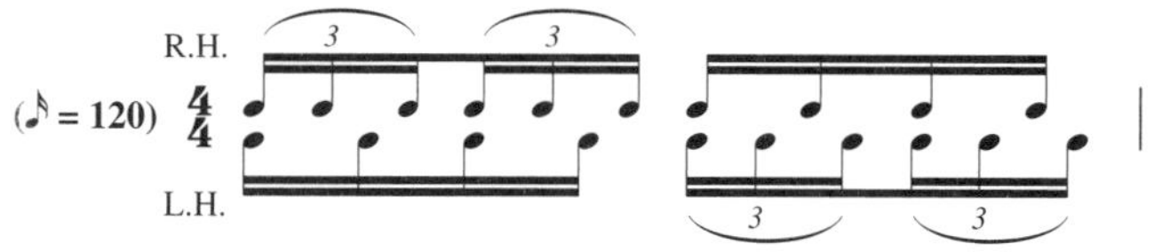 (♪ = 120)

381. 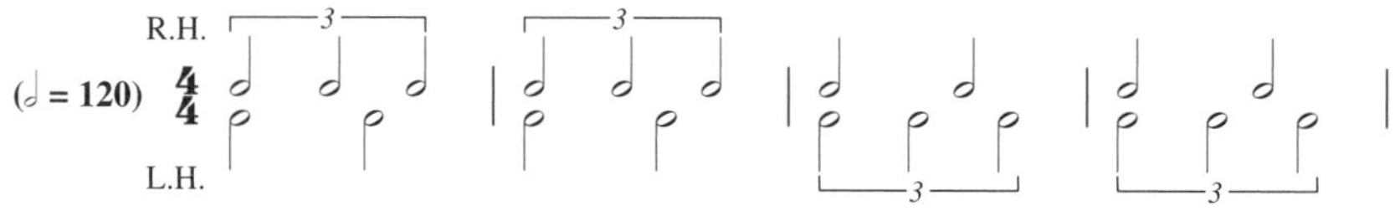 (♩ = 120)

Now, three against four:

382. 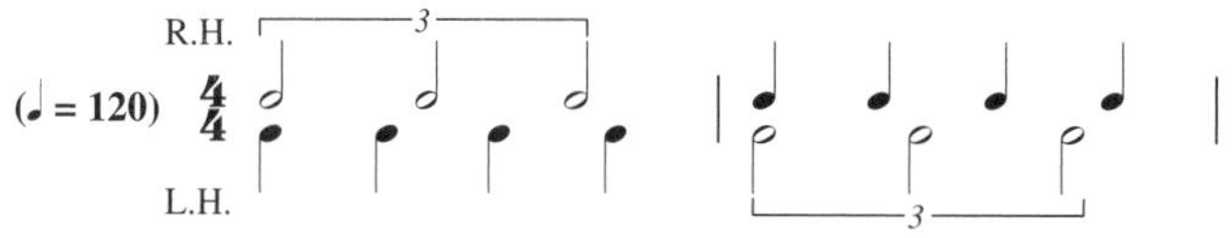 (♩ = 120)

Written as one line, the above becomes:

383.

Using the same principle, play:

384. 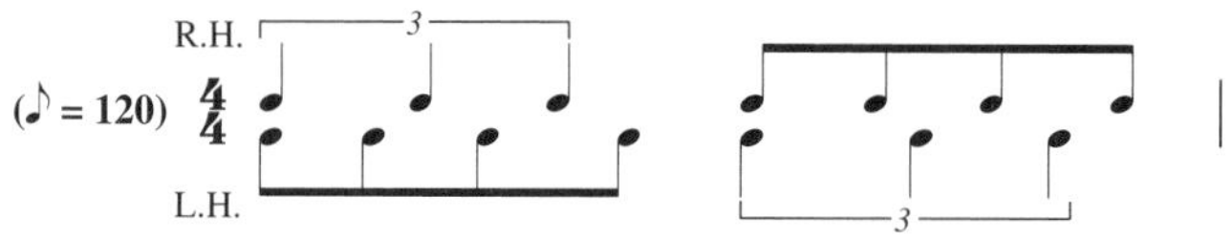 (♪ = 120)

385. 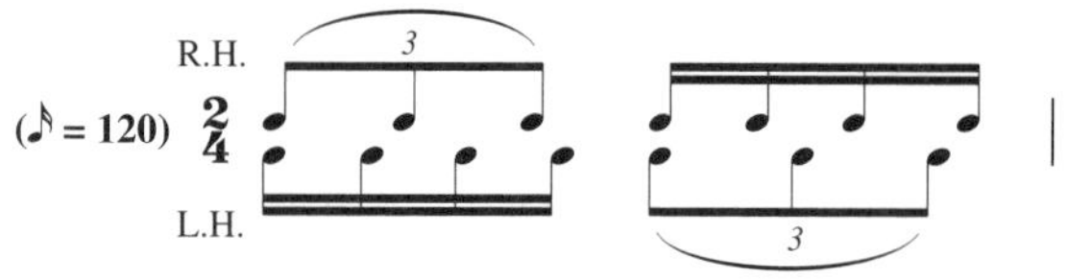 (♪ = 120)

HAND INDEPENDENCE USING TRIPLETS

In the following, it is necessary to maintain the right-hand cymbal beat in its triplet form ♩ ♫ ♩ ♫ . Each example is written two ways: each hand is written on a different space first, and immediately below this first line, the two hands are combined. In the second line, the flams indicate that both hands play simultaneously.

(In all the exercises in this section, the right hand plays a cymbal, the left the snare).

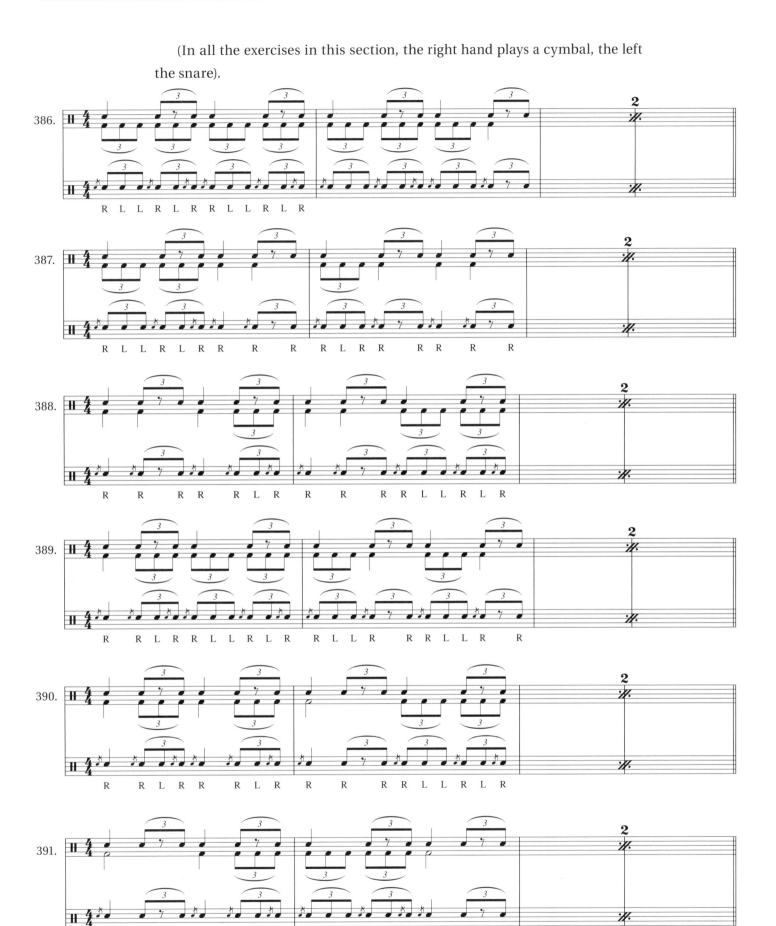

HAND INDEPENDENCE USING
EIGHTH AND SIXTEENTH NOTES

In the following examples, it is necessary that the right hand play the cymbal beat as a true dotted-eighth-and-sixteenth figure ♩ ♫♩ ♫ or ♩ ♫ ♩ ♫.

As before, the second stave is a one-line version of the first stave.

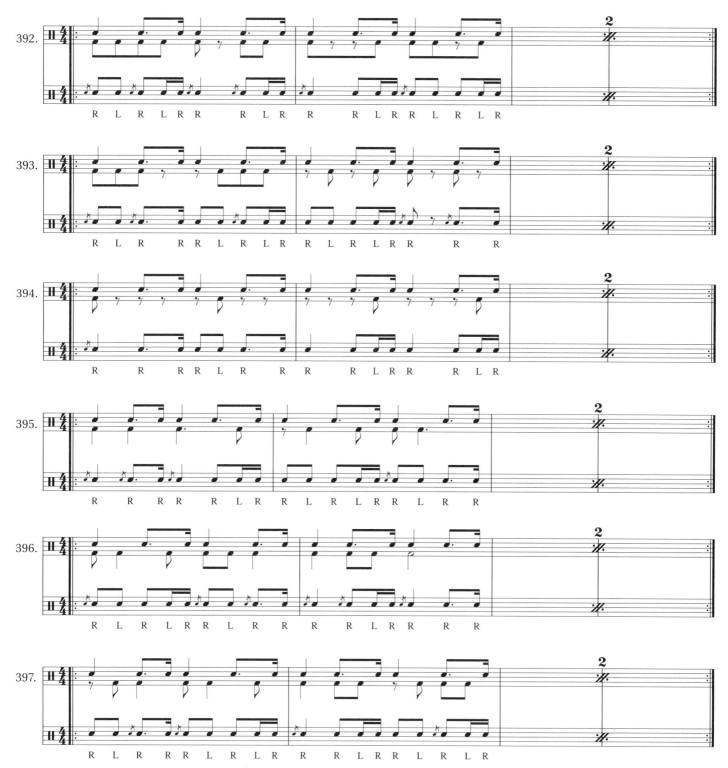

THE JAZZ DRUMMER AND THE DRUM SOLO

(The following is reprinted from the March 30, 1961 issue of *DownBeat* magazine with the permission of that magazine.)

EVOLUTION OF THE DRUM SOLO

By Don DeMicheal

All jazz is one. What is contemporary is of the past. There may be leaps forward, mad and rapid changes may occur, but there are no revolutions in jazz. Evolution, sí; revolution, no. There is a connection, a jazz "blood" line, between Johnny Dodds and Eric Dolphy, between young Louis Armstrong and young Lee Morgan, between Baby Dodds and Louis Hayes. The lines may be blurred and have taken circuitous routes from then to now, but lines there are.

How can these "blood" lines be recognized? Words and ear fail to convey fully the degree of unity. A more precise and visual method is needed. With all its possible weaknesses, musical notation is the only method available that would serve as a visual guide to musical evolution. By transcribing the work of the most influential musicians in the history of jazz or representatives of certain "schools," the ties and connections can be shown clearly.

Jazz theorists have long held the belief that jazzmen imitate, whether consciously or unconsciously, the sound of the human voice. The voice theory holds up well enough when applied to brasses, reeds, and strings. But it has seldom, if ever, been applied to percussion. The whole subject of vocalism in percussion has been studiously avoided. It need not be, for there are several vocal mannerisms to be found in jazz drumming.

Some drummers hum and sing while they solo. They are not always indulging in showmanship—they sing the rhythmic figures they play. Besides these who visibly "vocalize," there are many jazz drummers who acknowledge that some sort of melody goes through their minds while they solo. Some improvise around their own inaudible melodies.

But there is less-abstract evidence than this in jazz drumming to support the vocal theory. There is pitch variation obtained by utilizing the various drums and the many whackable accessories drummers use. The variations may be slight, but they parallel the pitch variations of human speech. The first jazz record, *Original Dixieland One-Step* by the Original Dixieland Jazz Band, contains evidence of percussion pitch variation: ODJB drummer Tony Sbarbaro (Spargo) played on what sounds like temple blocks and woodblocks, snare drum, and a Chinese tom-tom, each with a unique pitch and timbre.

The jazz drummer also imitates the cadence of speech, as do other instrumentalists. (It's no accident that the phrases, "Talk to me," "Shout," "Holler," "Now you're talkin'" and other speech references are a large part of jazz argot.) Early jazz drumming such as Sbarbaro's and Baby Dodds' contained little speech cadence, however. The military tradition, which tends to fill each measure with many notes, was too strong in their work to allow for the pauses characteristic of speech (or melody). It was not until orchestral drumming, which allows greater use of space, became a stronger influence than the military that jazz drumming came closer to speech cadence.

The military influence has not completely disappeared from jazz drumming, but its influence is much less now than it was in the formative years of jazz. Not until the 1930s did militarism in jazz give way to the orchestral, and then only grudgingly. The seeds of its weakening and the ascendancy of orchestral drumming have been present since primitive jazz, just as jazz as a whole has steadily drifted from the military and folk toward the orchestral (or classical). There is nothing new about Third Streamism. (There must be one qualification made, however: with the coming of greater social acceptance—far from ideal though it may be—and greater political power for the Negro, there has been a correlated upsurge in racial pride. Some jazzmen have attempted a return—without primitivism—to the Negro's heritage. But the path back has not included the military.)

Aside from these larger elements involved in jazz drumming, there are particular characteristics common to all styles of jazz drumming. One is syncopation.

Basic to all jazz, and most assuredly to the jazz drummer, is the ability to swing. This is beyond the scope of notation. Accents can be indicated, but it is impossible to indicate the volume of the accent. Swinging involves a vast variety of accents, all of different volume, all shaded in a different way. For instance, in transcribing these solos, we found that to notate a passage as straight eighth notes is not entirely accurate; there are small variations in volume from note to note. Some of the notes are slightly delayed or accelerated. These variations are impossible to notate with clarity. These variations are as individual as are speech variations. No two people speak exactly alike; no two jazzmen play exactly alike. Thus, the limitations of transcribing jazz, or any music, for that matter. But we feel the examples will convey to the student the essence of these solos and styles.

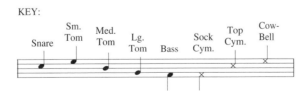

KEY:

Baby Dodds

Warren (Baby) Dodds was born in New Orleans around the turn of the century. His earliest recorded work was with the King Oliver Creole Jazz Band in the 1920s, but this example of his playing is from Stompy Jones, recorded in the late '30s with Sidney Bechet on Victor. Dodds displayed a subtle sense of pitch variation in his playing, although he remained under the influence of military drumming throughout his career. (He died in 1959.) He employed pitch variation by using an assortment of "traps." (In passing, there is no such thing as a "trap" drum. The term is an old nickname for the accessories the drummer carried: temple blocks, woodblocks, gongs, cymbals, cowbells, etc.). This solo excerpt was played on cowbell, woodblock, and the shell of the bass drum. The tempo is moderately fast with a two-beat feeling (i.e., the emphasis is on the first and third beat of the measure as opposed to a four-beat feeling, which emphasizes all four beats of the measure).

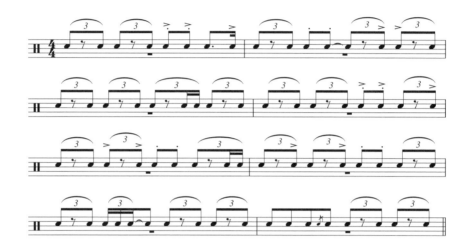

The example shows Dodds' adherence to the military mode of drumming: the measures are filled with notes played in a more-or-less evenly balanced manner. But there is an interesting mixing of triple ♪♪ and duple ♪♪ . Dodds mixed the two meters more subtly and intricately than did his followers. (Among others, Gene Krupa, Dave Tough, and George Wettling listened closely to Dodds when they were youngsters in Chicago.) Not until recently has there been more than a smidgen of this mixing—at least to the degree of complexity employed by Dodds.

Chick Webb

William (Chick) Webb was born in Baltimore, MD, only a few years after Dodds, but their styles, while both basically military-oriented, differed in devices used. Dodds was more subtle than Webb, but he did not have the flair of Webb. The small, crippled drummer (he died of tuberculosis in 1939) gained his greatest fame at the Savoy Ballroom during the late 1920s and throughout most of the '30s. Webb's band was the house band at the ballroom for many years and fought musical "battles " with other bands that played the Harlem dance palace. His influence is evident in the work of the drummers of the swing era. One of his most astute "students" was young Gene Krupa, who had left Chicago to go to New York City in 1929.

The following example is not from any of his recorded work but was written by George Wettling and appeared in his "Tips to Tubmen" column in *DownBeat* years ago; it also was published in Wettling's drum method, *America's Great*

Drum Stylists, published by Capitol Songs, Inc., in 1945. It is a close approximation of Webb's style. Wettling marked the solo to be played at a fast tempo.

Militarism is dominant but there is a wide use of pitch variation. The interplay between tom-tom, snare, cymbal, and cowbell, while not as subtle as Dodds' use of "traps," is brilliant. But the big difference between Dodds and Webb was in the "feel" of the time. Webb—notice the bass drum—played with a four-beat feeling, while Dodds usually did not.

Gene Krupa

Krupa is the most famous drummer in jazz—at least among non-musicians. One of the group of young Chicagoans who were taken with the music played by the early jazz pioneers, he rose to prominence with the Benny Goodman Band in the middle and late '30s—the swing era. Derided by critics and fellow musicians for his sometimes extroverted showmanship, Krupa, nonetheless, is important for his musical contributions to jazz drumming. His influence extends even to this day. Learning from the two masters, Dodds and Webb, Krupa simplified Dodds' complexity, but he still retained the militarism of the earlier style. The example is taken from Krupa's solo on the Benny Goodman Trio's version of *Who?*, recorded on Victor during the mid-'30s. He plays brushes throughout.

The tempo is brisk, staccato notes are played as straight eighth notes.

There is a similarity in general construction between Krupa's solo and Dodds'. There is no bass drum used. (Most of Krupa's solos used little bass drum.) There is internal use of duple and triple (measures 3 and 4); the measures are balanced. These are characteristic also of the Dodds' solo. But Krupa, unlike Dodds, usually played with a four-beat feeling, like Webb.

Buddy Rich

The best of those who followed in the path Krupa had blazed and who paralleled him in style and career was Bernard (Buddy) Rich. Son of show business parents, he began drumming at an extremely early age, was a solo act when he was 6, and led his own band at the age of 11. He gained fame as a jazz drummer by his exciting work with Artie Shaw and Tommy Dorsey bands in the swing era. Many contend that Rich is probably the best drummer in the world. That is not to say the best jazz drummer; there are no "bests." But for playing the instrument, there are none who surpass Rich. He may lack finesse and restraint at times, but there are few fellow drummers who do not acknowledge his technical, though not necessarily conceptual, superiority.

The example of Rich's soloing (from "Cheek to Cheek" in his Argo album *Playtime*) is played at an extremely fast tempo. Although recorded recently, the solo is within the military-conception focus—an overall balance from measure to measure, and non-"melodic" in conception (although Rich is capable of playing quite "melodically").

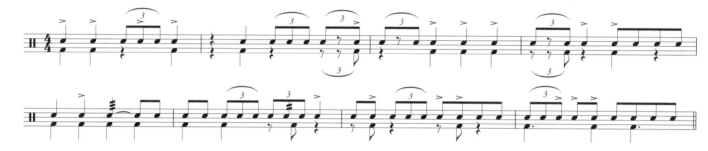

Another feature of the solo and Rich's playing in general is his accenting, which gives his work great vitality. Notable also is his mixing of eighth notes and triplets.

Cozy Cole

William (Cozy) Cole is from East Orange, N. J., and has been playing since he was a child (he even fashioned his own drumsticks in a manual training school). First inspired by Duke Ellington percussionist ("drummer" is an unsatisfactory term in this case) Sonny Greer, Cole gained fame with his work with the Cab Calloway Band of the late '30s. Cole was particularly known for his solos on the Calloway recordings of "Paradiddle Joe" and "Ratamacue."

An admirably facile drummer and, like Gene Krupa, an advocate of rudimental drumming—an integral part of military drumming—Cole is capable of executing solos of the greatest complexity utilizing hand-and-foot independence. The example shown does not include this device, which in simplified form is used extensively in modern drumming, but on paper it would look something like this:

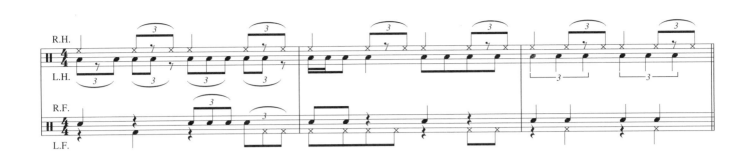

The transcribed example of Cole's work is excerpted from his solo on "Cole Heat, Warm Feet" recorded by the Hank D'Amico Quartet in the middle 1940s on National Records. The tempo is brisk. Cole plays with a 12/8 feeling here. He obtained an intriguing effect by muffling the snare (bottom) head of his snare drum—or else, the head was broken.

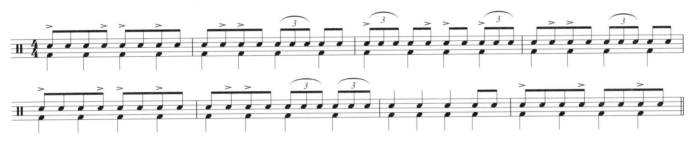

The direction of the solo is almost completely military, but the accenting breaks up the flow of notes. The example is noticeably void of rests.

Sid Catlett

Big Sid, born in Evansville, IN;, was one of the most highly regarded drummers in jazz. He came to prominence with his big-band work with Louis Armstrong in the late '30s, but his finest work was done in the '40s. When he died of a heart attack at the age of 41 in 1951, traditionalists and modernists alike mourned him.

The heavy military and the gaining-in-strength orchestral influences met handsomely in Catlett. The use of space, heard often in orchestral drum work, is evident in Catlett's playing. But more importantly, Catlett brought a more "melodic" concept to jazz drumming. There was melodiousness in jazz drumming before him, but it was covered with the military. It took the form generally of pitch variation between different drums and "traps." Catlett retained pitch variation but added speech cadence—melodiousness, if you want—to jazz drum literature. He set riffs in opening statements, sometimes repeating them for several bars, then embellished them. He played little "tunes." He varied the pitch of rim shots (in the example, the rim shots marked as accents in the first two bars—and subsequent repeats of the figure—each had a different sound, one impossible to intimate on paper).

The 12-bar Catlett solo, one of his best, is taken from "1-2-3 Blues," recorded about 1946 by his own group for Session Records. It is played at a medium tempo.

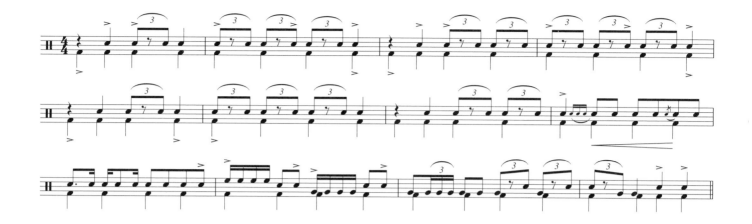

The beauty of this solo lies in its construction. First Catlett plays a two-bar statement, repeats it until the eighth bar, then builds to a climax in the eleventh bar, resolving the solo in the final bar with two emphatic accents, clearing the way for the tenor saxophone solo of Ben Webster, which follows the drum solo.

We will deviate from chronology in order to show the extent of Catlett's direct influence. (His indirect influence has stemmed from the emulation by young drummers of such men as Kenny Clarke, Shelly Manne, Max Roach, and Art Blakey.)

Philly Joe Jones

Joseph Rudolph (Philly Joe) Jones became widely known among jazzmen by his work in his native Philadelphia during the 1940s, but it was not until he joined Miles Davis on a more-or-less regular basis in the 1950s that he became known to the jazz public.

Philly Joe continues the Catlett tradition perhaps in a more nearly pure form than any other modern drummer. (The tie between Jones and Catlett is not only musical but personal as well. Catlett, according to Jones, willed Philly Joe his favorite cymbals, which Jones has mounted in a place of honor in his home.) The conceptual similarity between the two is evident in Jones' "melodiousness."

The following excerpt was transcribed from "Joe's Debut" in the Riverside album *Philly Joe Jones Showcase*, issued in 1960. The tempo is just a little faster than that of the Catlett example. The solo is played with a slight 12/8 feeling.

The solo is constructed in the Catlett manner: opening statement (in this case two statements, bars 1-4 and 5-8), followed by embellishment (not shown in the example but following those first eight measures, on the record). The excerpt is notable for other reasons as well: the use of space, simple antiphony, and the extended use of the figure  . This figure seems to be common to all styles of jazz drumming. It is found—although covered and surrounded by other notes—in the Dodds (third and fifth measures), the Krupa (third measure), the Cole (first, fifth, and eighth measures), and the Catlett (second, fourth, sixth, and ninth measures) examples, as well as in some of those following.

Kenny Clarke

Kenneth (Klook) Clarke was one of the charter members of the group of musicians in the early 1940s who were later to be known as the "boppers"— the spearheads of jazz modernity. But Clark was well-known among musicians before the advent of bop; he worked with the bands of Roy Eldridge, Claude Hopkins, and Teddy Hill, among others, in the '30s. He recorded with Sidney Bechet during that decade and made his first trip to Europe, where he now lives, in 1937. He was leader of the house band at Minton's Playhouse in the formative period of bop. Sometimes credited with the founding of bop (or klook-mop) drumming, he was quite influential among young drummers, including Max Roach, in the early '40s. His use of the bass drum, and non-use of the bass drum, were widely copied. Still, there is a detectable Catlettness about his playing.

The example of Clarke's solo work is taken from "Opus and Interlude" in the Milt Jackson album *Opus de Funk* on Savoy Records, recorded in the mid '50s. The example consists of four four-bar breaks played at a medium tempo.

Max Roach

As influential as Catlett and Clarke were, their direct influence pales when compared to that of the drummer who best learned the lessons they offered—Max Roach. Roach has been the most influential drummer since Krupa, and like Krupa, he popularized (among musicians) a style that grew from two predecessors, in his case, Catlett and Clarke. But he took these basic conception tools and fashioned his own way of playing. There are still evidences of his mentors' influence in his work, but Roach is his own man, make no mistake about it. He has been one of the real explorers in jazz drumming. Not content to stand still, but continually seeking new, more challenging frontiers, Roach has continued to evolve throughout his career. Groups under his leadership were among the first to play jazz in 3/4; he is now doing extensive exploration in 5/4.

The solo excerpt is from Charlie Parker's recording of "Koko" made for Savoy Records in the mid '40s. The tempo is very fast.

Where Catlett and others usually thought in terms of two-bar phrases, Roach, as seen in the example, worked more with four-bar phrases. Note the similarity between the first two four-bar phrases. His accents, which fall mostly on the last note of three-note groups, give his playing an internal symmetry but, coextensively, lend a general asymmetry to the solo. Clear? In other words, the solo has internal balance but external imbalance. While "melodiousness" as exemplified by the works of Catlett and, later, Philly Joe Jones, is missing from the "Koko" solo, Roach played melodically in some of his early work (e.g., "Salt Peanuts" with Dizzy Gillespie) and has increased his use of vocalism in his current work, although the use takes the form of speech more than "singing."

Shelly Manne

Manne, son of a well-known percussionist in New York City, gained his first recognition by his fine work on records with men like Coleman Hawkins and Eddie Heywood. He leaped to wider recognition, among both musicians and public, by the excellence of his work with the early Stan Kenton bands in the middle and late '40s. He was one of the leading drummers in the so-called West Coast movement of the '50s.

Always a colorist, melodic drumming is a large element in his work—he has been known to tune his drums to a definite pitch in order to play melody in the true sense of the phrase. He has had great influence, especially among the drummers on the West Coast. Originally a player in the Catlett mode (as evidenced by his early recording efforts), he came under the influence of bop in the '40s, with a style similar to Max Roach's. But the stay with Kenton and his subsequent move to California had an effect on his playing, and he developed it to a high artistic level.

The example is excerpted from the duo album he made in 1954 with pianist Russ Freeman on the Contemporary label. (It has recently been reissued.) One of the important drum records, it contains some of the best Manne drumming on records. This example is from Manne's second solo (with sticks) on the track "Sound Effects Manne." It is played with a slight 12/8 feeling at a medium-fast tempo.

Manne's use of space in the first two measures and the pitch-variation effects throughout are notable features of the excerpt. There is also a sparing use of bass drum.

Frank Isola

Isola, underrated and unrecognized, is an excellent drummer, though he cannot be put in the same class as Dodds, Catlett, Krupa, Roach, etc., in regards to influence (the mark of greatness). But he is included in this study not only because of the excellence of his work during the 1950s with the groups of Stan Getz and Gerry Mulligan but because he is representative of the so-called "cool" school of jazz drumming. Stemming from the spacious playing of Manne and Chico Hamilton, the cool school reached its zenith in the mid '50s.

Cool drumming is marked by the simplicity of few notes played but the complexity of odd groupings of notes and intricate combinations of snare, bass, tom-toms, and cymbals. The example of Isola's work is from "Feather Merchant," included in the Norgran album *Stan Getz at the Shrine*. The eight-bar example is made up of two four-bar breaks played by Isola in exchange with trombonist Bob Brookmeyer. In a way, this is quoting Isola out of context, since his breaks were like extensions of Brookmeyer's ideas. The solos are at a medium-bounce tempo and have a feeling of 12/8.

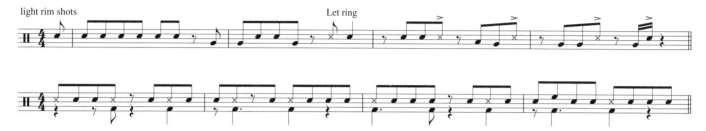

The examples are marked by the grace and swing that Isola brought to his work during this period. The cymbals are struck lightly near the center, getting a "ping" sound, and are allowed to ring. The examples are notable for the use of space and three-note groups.

Art Blakey

The blaze of neo-bop, or hard bop, heated the jazz scene in the middle and late '50s. The most fiery of the hard-bop drummers is undoubtedly the volcanic Art Blakey. Though he came into prominence only in the last decade, Blakey has been a respected jazzman since the late 1930s when he joined the band of Fletcher Henderson. He was the drummer from 1944-47 in the legendary Billy Eckstine Band, which at different times was filled with such excellent musicians as Charlie Parker, Dizzy Gillespie, Shorts McConnell, Dexter Gordon, Gene Ammons, Fats Navarro, Miles Davis, and Sarah Vaughan. In the early 1950s, Blakey was a featured sideman in the Buddy DeFranco Quartet. Since 1955, he has headed his own group, with varying personnel, under the name of the Jazz Messengers. Some of his most interesting drum work is contained in the albums he has made for Blue Note with African and Cuban drummers.

Following the path of Catlett-Clarke-Roach, Blakey injected a west-African flavor into much of his work. His use of odd note-groupings (seven and five quarter notes played against four quarter notes), the superimposition of 6/4 over 4/4, asymmetry, and great use of space are hallmarks of his work. One of the most easily identifiable characteristics of his playing is an ever-present, strongly played sock cymbal on the afterbeats. Many young hard-bop drummers have been heavily influenced by Blakey.

The example of Blakey's solo work was transcribed from his solo on "Paper Moon" in his Blue Note album, *The Big Beat.* The tempo is fast.

Of all the examples included in this study, Blakey's is the most spacious. After the cymbal crash at the beginning of the solo, nothing is heard except the fading cymbal and the sock cymbal for three bars, then there is a short flurry of notes followed by more space. This construction is used again, but the space becomes less and less, until finally, the solo is filled with notes (the measures following the excerpt).

There are many young drummers of awesome talent, who, while they have not yet proved to be as significant to the course of jazz drumming as men like Dodds, Krupa, Webb, Catlett, Clarke, Roach, and Manne, nevertheless may be the trailblazers of tomorrow's jazz. Among those of promise, and this list does not include all, are Louis Hayes, with an unquenchable fire in his playing; Joe Morello, melodic and irrepressibly humorous; Art Taylor, full of drive; Ed Thigpen, tasty and restrained; Billy Higgins; Jimmy Cobb; Albert Heath; Eddie Blackwell; Pete LaRoca; Dannie Richmond, and Elvin Jones.

Perhaps one of them or some young drummer yet unknown will be the one to abstract from the past and shape the future. For surely the "blood lines" will extend from past to future; the ties will be there. Thus the unity of jazz, thus its greatness.

DEVELOPING THE ABILITY TO PLAY MUSICAL DRUM SOLOS

This section is made up mostly of what some would call "exercises." They are not designed as exercises per se but as a means to an end—a stimulation, if you will, that the authors hope will goad the student to use his own imagination. *Do not memorize any of these examples.* Play them, study them, combine them, if you want, but use your own mind when playing solos. Your solo must express *you*, not a book or a mechanical pattern.

And when that time comes when you play a solo or exchange four- or eight-bar phrases with another musician, make that solo or those exchanges flow out and into what comes before and after. Continue the musical thought laid down for you, perhaps turn the direction of that thought, but do not destroy the thought. At the risk of seeming lunatic on this point, we, the authors scream at you, "PLAY MUSIC!"

BASS/SNARE COMBINATIONS

The following bass-snare combinations are arranged in four-bar phrases, but they can be practiced different ways. For instance, instead of reading across, read down, playing the first bar of each phrase; then read the first and second bars of each line, and so forth.

(For these examples, the bass drum is written with the stem of the note up, instead of down. It makes the examples easier to read. The snare drum may be played with either hand.)

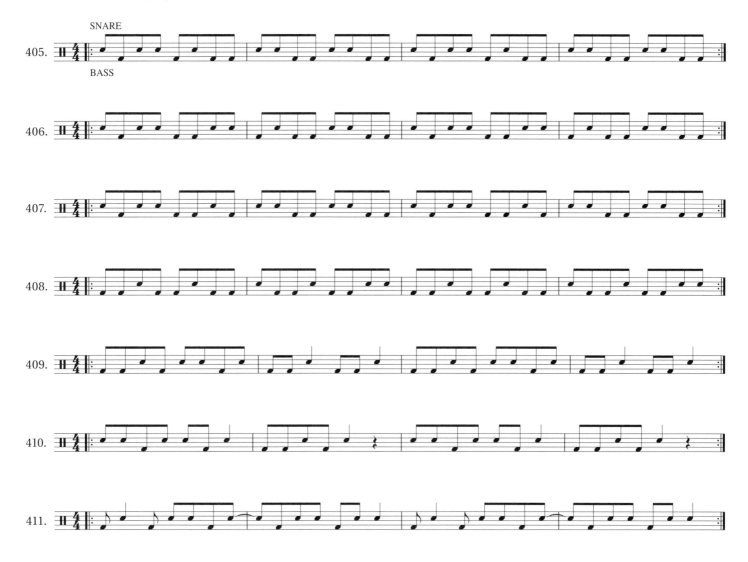

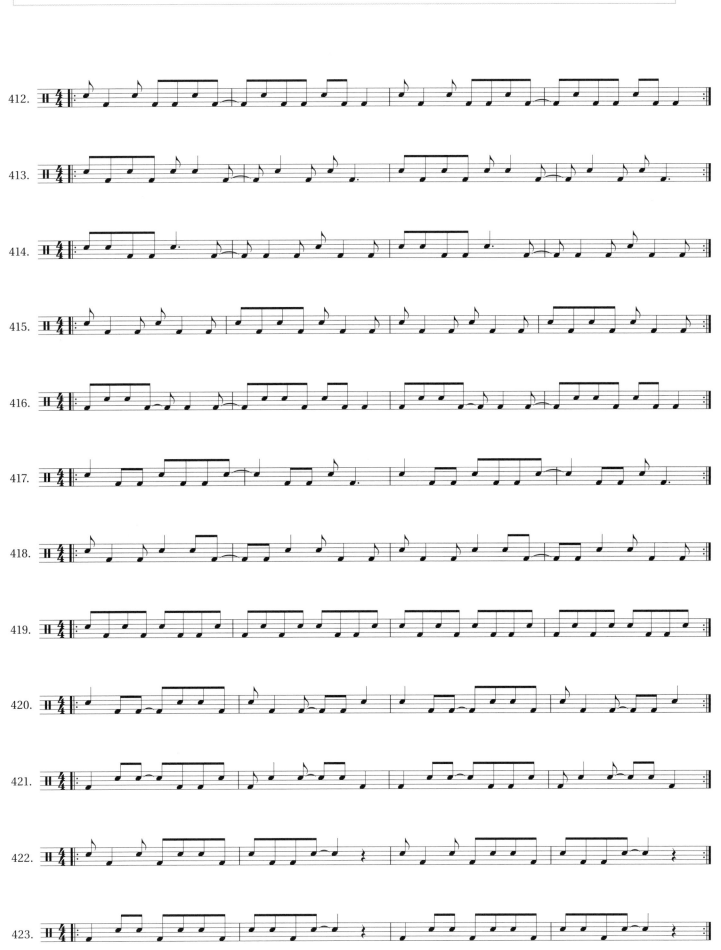

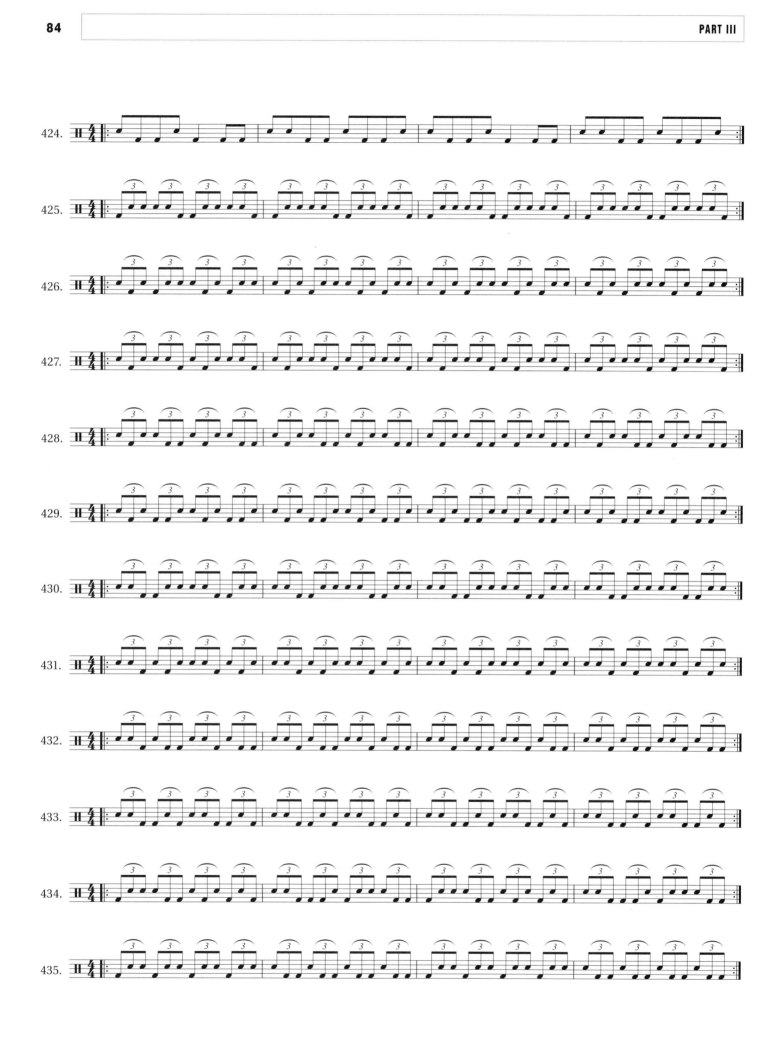

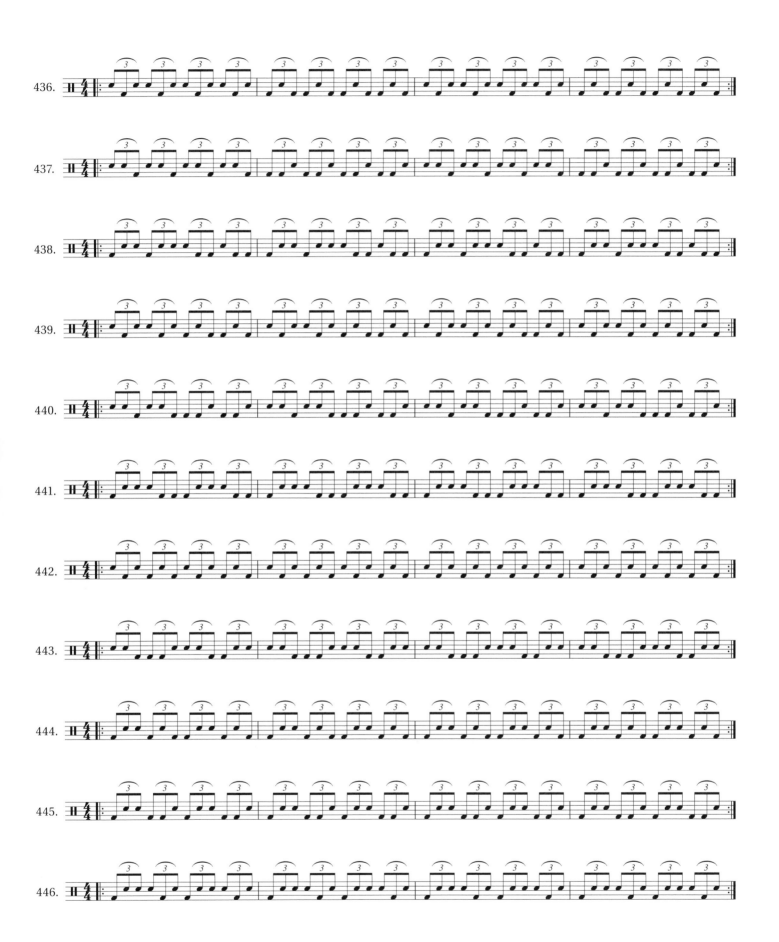

SNARE/TOM-TOM COMBINATIONS

Below are examples of snare/tom-tom combinations. Note sticking. Keep time with bass drum and hi-hat.

Hand-to-Hand Sticking Combinations

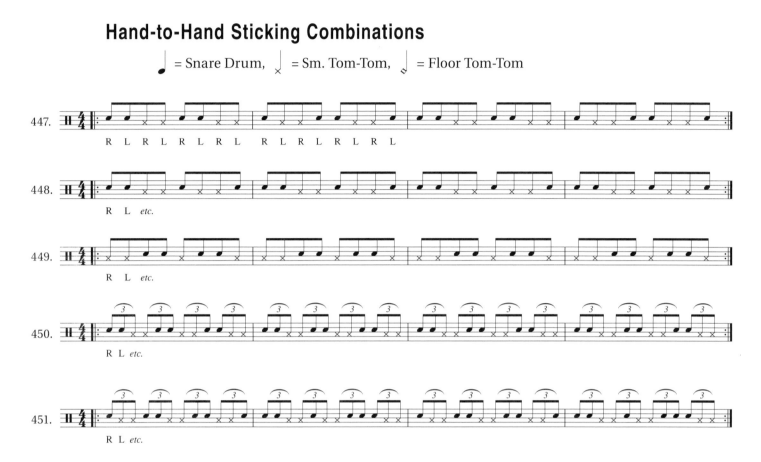

Single, Double, and Triple Paradiddle Combinations

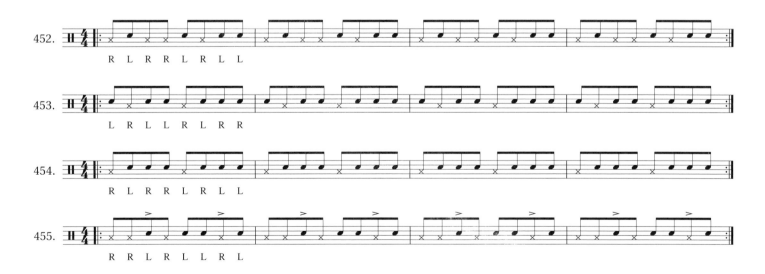

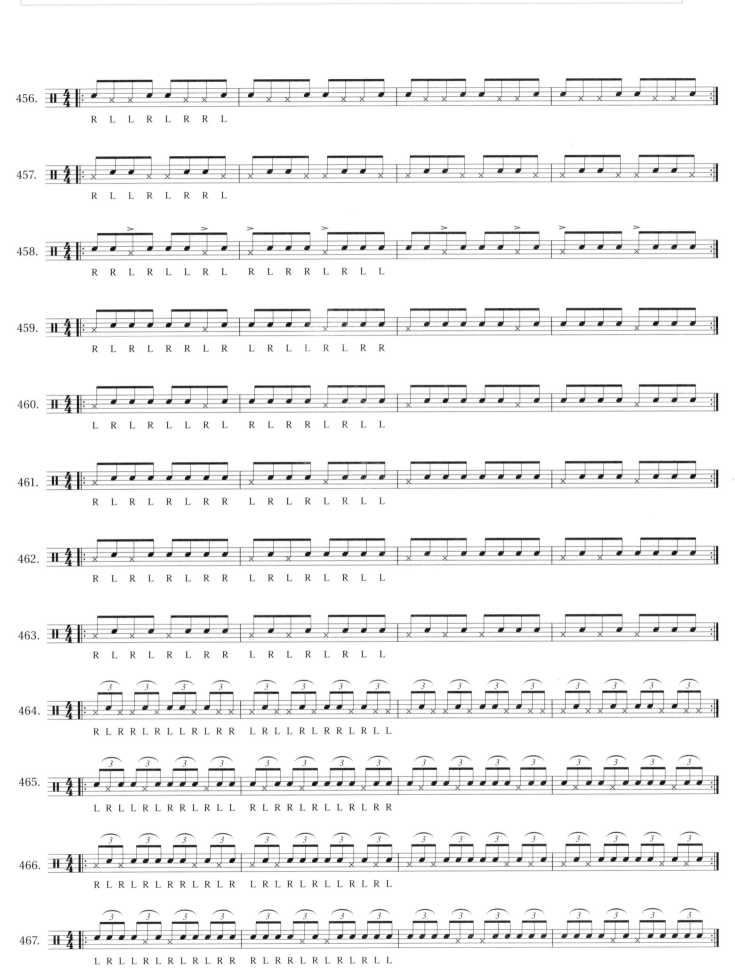

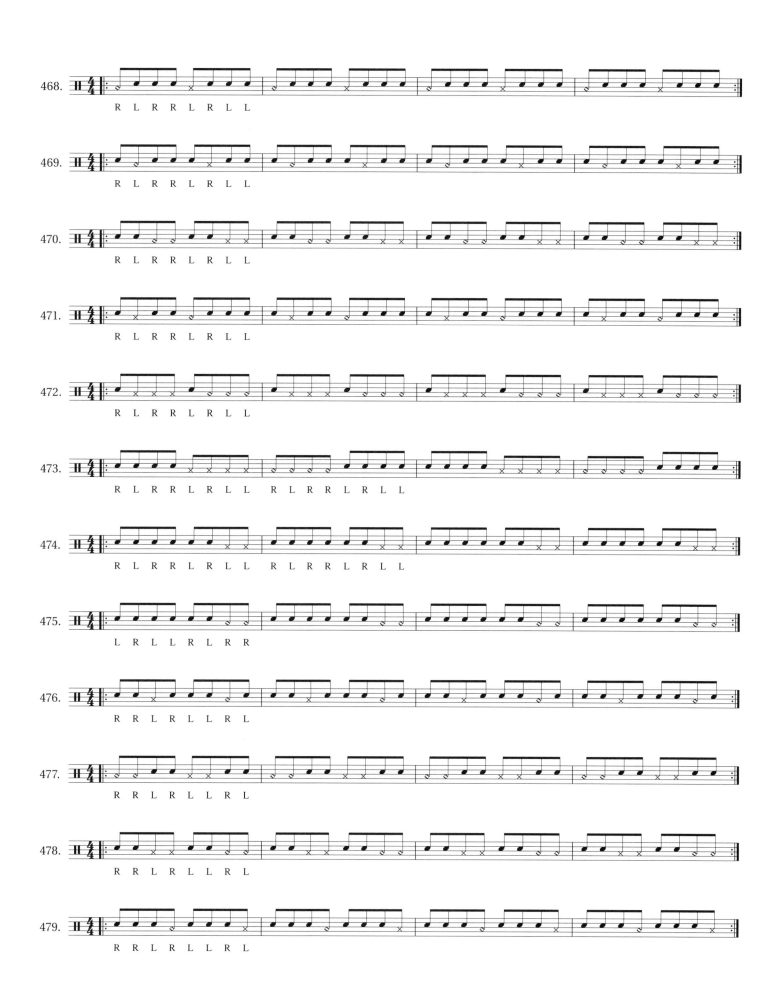

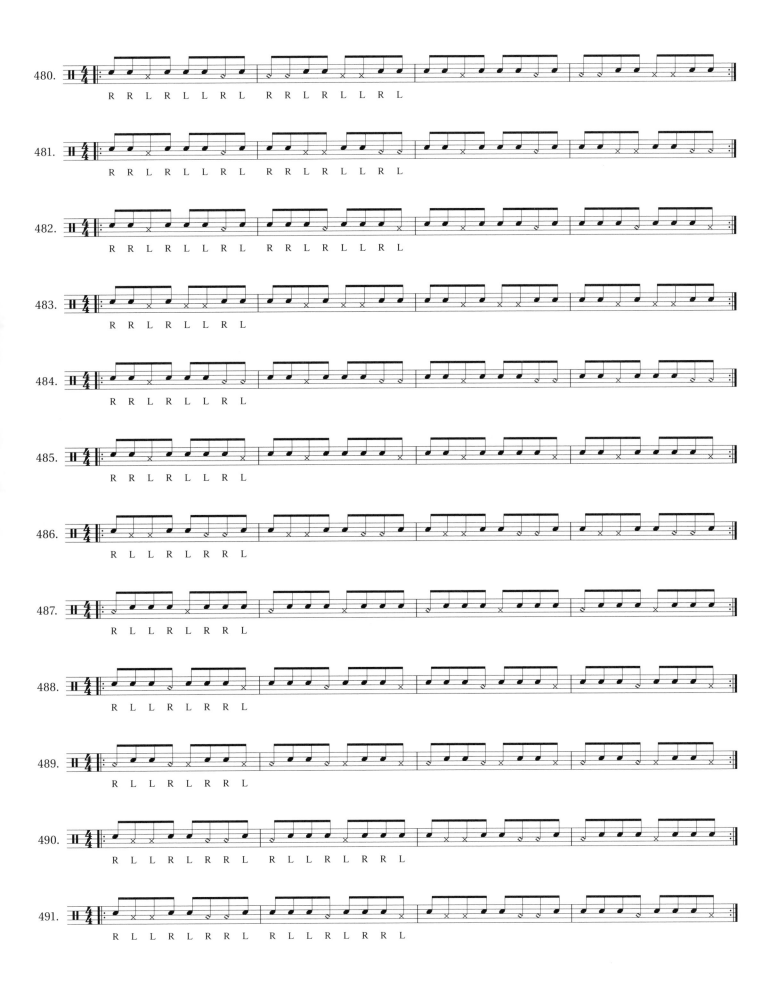

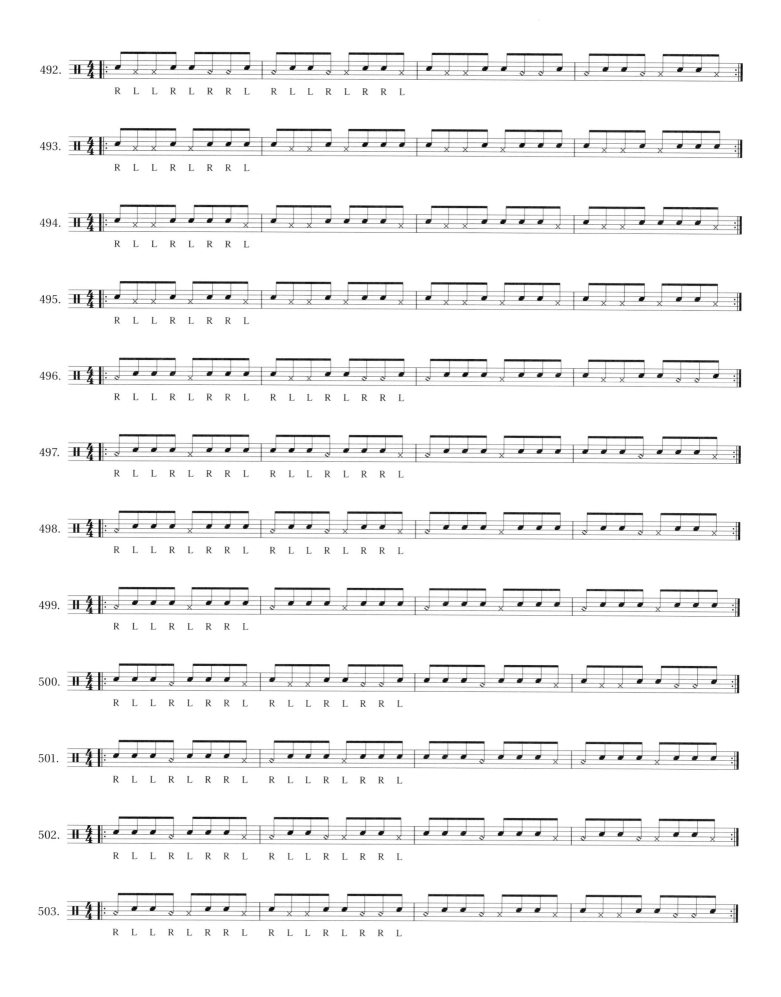

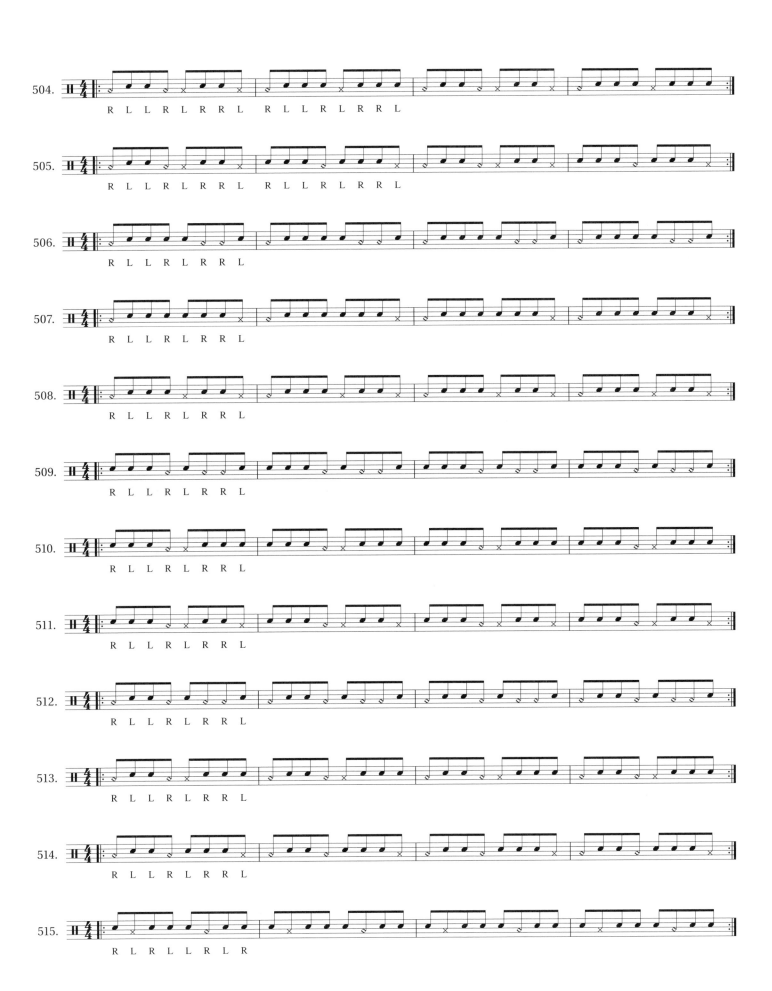

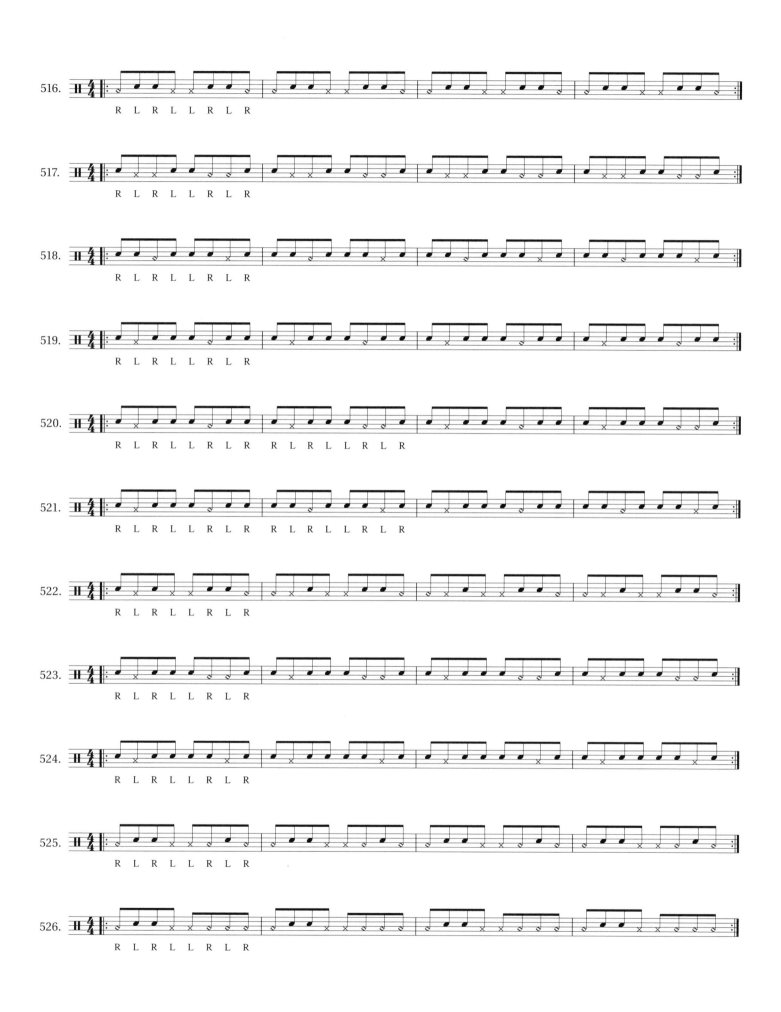

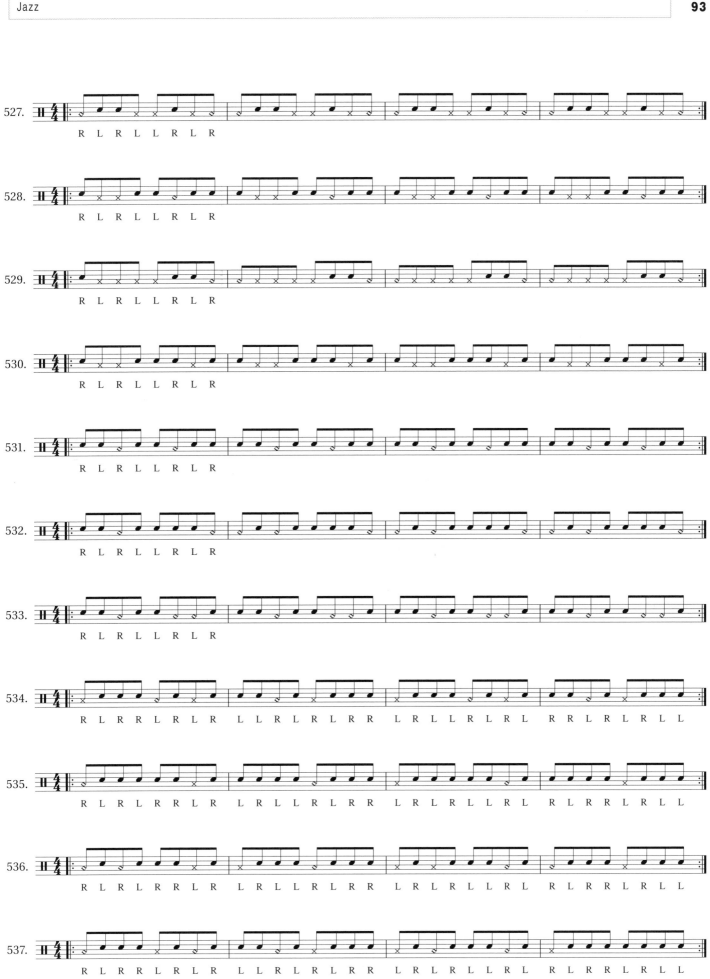

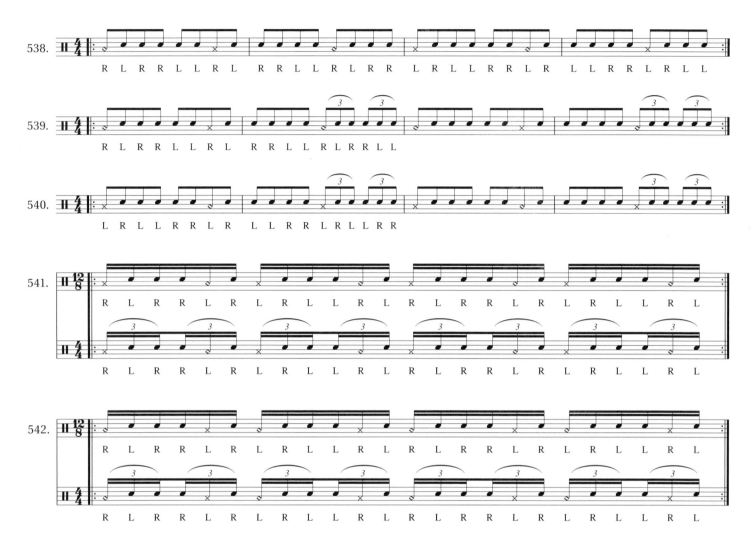

After you understand this section, after you have become accustomed to moving around the set, compose your own solos. Make them musical. Make them make sense.

CONCLUSION

We hope you have gained insight into the intricacies of dance-band jazz drumming by your study of this book. We fervently hope you have become aware of the musical possibilities of drums and will apply what you have learned when you go into the professional music world.

Of course, no book is an end-all. This one certainly was not written with this in mind. The authors' only purpose in writing this book was to furnish the novice with what we consider the basic knowledge any drummer should have. We have tried to impart our great concern that the drummer should at all times be musical. If only this one thing has become clear, the book has justified its existence.

ABOUT THE AUTHORS

Alan Dawson

Photo Courtesy of Zildjian Corp.

George Alan Dawson (1929 to 1996) was born on July 14, 1929 in Marietta, Pennsylvania. He was the fourth child born to the late James W. and Eva Dawson. Alan was raised in Roxbury, Massachusetts. By the tender age of fourteen, he was playing professionally.

He studied drum set for four years with percussionist Charles Alden before serving in the Army in 1951 during the Korean War. Alan played with the Army Dance Band while stationed at Fort Dix. After his release from the Army in 1953, he toured for three months in Europe with the Lionel Hampton Orchestra. He then returned to Roxbury and began working with his former boss, local bandleader, Sabby Lewis.

There have been many honors in Alan's illustrious fifty-year jazz career. During the mid-fifties, he was able to maintain an active recording career including clinics and some brief tours. In 1957, he became the house drummer for six nights a week at Wally's Paradise in Boston. He also began his eighteen-year teaching career at Berklee College of Music.

In the early sixties, Alan joined pianist, Ray Santisi and bassist, John Neves, as the house rhythm section at Lennie's on the Turnpike in Peabody, Massachusetts, where the wider world discovered his talent.

Alan recorded with such greats as Booker Ervin, Dave Brubeck, Lionel Hampton, Quincy Jones, George Benson, Clifford Brown, Jaki Byard, James Williams, Andy McGhee, Phil Wilson, Bill Pierce, John Lockwood, and many more. He traveled extensively in this country as well as Europe, Australia, and Asia.

Alan was a pioneering jazz drum teacher at Berklee College of Music, where he taught from 1957 to 1975, and his influence continues, with courses and teaching approaches echoing his influence decades after his passing. Among some of his notable pupils are Harvey Mason, Terri Lyne Carrington, Jake Hanna, Kenwood Dennard, Tony Williams, Keith Copeland, Bobby Ward, Akira Tara, and many others.

Alan's work with Jaki Byard on piano and Richard Davis on bass for Prestige records was substantial between 1963 and 1968. From 1968 to 1975, he worked with the Dave Brubeck Quartet and toured with Brubeck's family band, Two

Generations of Brubeck. In 1975, he ended his teaching at Berklee and worked out of his home until his death in 1996. This was also the period when he formed a quartet that included Bill Pierce, James Williams, and Richard Reid.

Alan and Florence Howell were married in 1954 after she completed nursing school. They had two children, Alan R. and Deborah Dawson Mullins, and three grandchildren, Melinda, Melvin Richard, and Alan R. Dawson, Jr.

Don DeMicheal

Photo Courtesy of
DownBeat magazine

Don DeMicheal (1928 to 1982) was a drummer, vibraphonist, and music journalist. While he is probably best known as a writer and editor for *DownBeat* magazine, DeMicheal was co-leader and vibraphonist of the Don DeMicheal-Chuck Hedges Swingtet, and a drummer in the Hot Three with Art Hodes on piano and Kenny Davern on clarinet.

From 1961 to 1967, DeMicheal was the editor-in-chief of *DownBeat* magazine. He is considered one of the greatest writer/editors in *DownBeat* history, known for being a fair-minded mastermind behind some of the magazine's most famous articles.

For example, in the Jan. 27, 1962, issue of *DownBeat*, it was DeMicheal's idea to have two critics review the hotly debated release of Ornette Coleman's *Free Jazz*. The result has become jazz history. Critic Pete Welding gave *Free Jazz* five stars in a glowing review, while critic John Tynan argued that the disc deserved ZERO stars. Those two reviews perfectly captured how fans and musicians alike reacted to Coleman and his dramatic break with jazz tradition.

DeMicheal also championed the music of John Coltrane, penning classic articles like "Coltrane On Coltrane" in the Sept. 29, 1960 issue and "John Coltrane and Eric Dolphy Answer the Jazz Critics," in the April 17, 1962 edition.

Even after his departure from *DownBeat*, DeMicheal served as a leader in the jazz community. He was president of the Jazz Institute of Chicago from 1974 to 1978, serving as program chair for the first Chicago Jazz Festival in Grant Park in 1979.

In 1981, DeMicheal played drums with Hodes and cornetist Wild Bill Davidson at Carnegie Hall in New York. The performance was part of a program called "Goin' to Chicago," which took the history of Chicago jazz into the heart of the Big Apple's Kool Jazz Festival.